To Anita & Fred
with love & very best wishes
Hope you enjoy the 'read'
                    Bill
                16/04/2010

BOW BELLS
to
BOREHAM WOOD

by

BILL O'NEILL

"The First Twenty Five Years of My Life,

from Childhood in London's Docklands,

to Manhood in Boreham Wood"

Growing up during the 1930s and 1940s

PUBLISHED BY ELSTREE & BOREHAM WOOD MUSEUM

First published by

Elstree and Boreham Wood Museum in 2010

Published by Elstree and Boreham Wood Museum

1 Drayton Road, Borehamwood

Hertfordshire   WD6 2DA

www.elstree-museum.co.uk

email: office@elstree-museum.co.uk

ISBN 978-0-9565297-0-1

Printed in Great Britain by the

MPG Books Group, Bodmin and King's Lynn

01553 764728

ACKNOWLEDGEMENTS

Jim Read	Recollections
Joe and Cissy Brady	Recollections
Derek Allen	Photos
The Island History Trust	Photos
Jean Atherton	Typing
Liz Stoneman	Photos
Elstree and Boreham Wood Museum	Photos

The contributors of illustrations and photos used in this book are shown against each picture.

Contents

INTRODUCTION

Having made contact with Alan Lawrence at the Elstree and Boreham Wood Museum in Drayton Road in 2005 about my book on the history of Boreham Wood Football Club and looking at many photographs of Boreham Wood and district it made me think about the Boreham Wood that I knew from 1941 so I decided to put into print my memories of those early days. I mentioned this to Alan and one of the points he raised was to put in as many names as I can remember and, if possible, where they lived because this helped considerably when tracing family names and connections. My first thoughts were to detail all of the shops in Shenley Road at the time.

It was also about this time that Jim Read contacted me about obtaining a copy of my book. We of course went down memory lane and he sent me a list of the shops etc. in Shenley Road (1941) as he remembered them. So with his permission I have used the list of shops and just added my observations. Jim also sent me a write up of his life and times in Boreham Wood and it is uncanny to see how our lives ran parallel all that time ago. Jim is the eldest son of Jim Read Snr. who owned the greengrocers next door to Hanson's taking over from Gillham's. We both came from the East End of London living within three miles of each other. We were both in the Kent hopfields when war broke out. We arrived in Boreham Wood within three weeks of each other to escape the bombing. We both had jobs as butchers' boys, he with Hunts and me with Tompkins. We worked at Elm Farm Dairies together. He served with the Home Guard and I 'fought' against him as an Army Cadet. We both married in All Saints' Church in Shenley Road. We both worked in the fully fashioned department of Keystone Knitting Mills, and were made redundant together In 1952, we started evening classes in maths together, we both got jobs as electronic wiremen, Jim with a firm in Radlett and me with Elliotts' in the Elstree Way. During the early eighties when he was between jobs Jim painted my house in Cowley Hill and one of my very good friends over many years was his Uncle George who I wrote about in my book on the history of Boreham Wood Football Club. Sixty six years later we are still in touch.

Another long standing friend of us both, Joe Brady, jogged my memory several times while I was preparing this write up, especially about Keystones. I first met Joe in 1942 and we both married local girls who had been friends since infant school in Shenley. In October 2006, Joe and Cissy Brady visited us in Shoeburyness for an overnight stay and the four of us never stopped talking as memories were recalled. During April 2007 we were in Bournemouth and on the way home visited Jim and Connie Read in their home in Christchurch for many more memories to be recalled.

I have produced this booklet which includes these memories and also others of the time before I came to live with my family in Boreham Wood in 1941 after we had been bombed out twice during the London Blitz. I was born in Millwall on the Isle of Dogs in 1927 and until our house was bombed early on in the Blitz had lived all of my life in West Ferry Road. When war broke out, many of our relatives were also living on the Island although a couple of aunts and uncles had moved away before the War, for which we would later be thankful. When we were made homeless by the bombing it was my Aunt in Becontree who provided us with accommodation, and then towards the end of the Blitz when our Becontree home was bombed, it was our Aunt in Boreham Wood who would help to find us a new home. Fortunately no further bombs dropped onto the O'Neills and I remained in Boreham Wood until I moved to my current home in Shoeburyness, Essex. The first twenty years of my life were some of the most enjoyable, traumatic, frightening and exciting that I have experienced. I hope that you will enjoy reading about them and, if you are old enough, will be reminded of some of the events.

Have a good read.

Bill O'Neill

PART 1

1927-1941

THE LONDON ERA

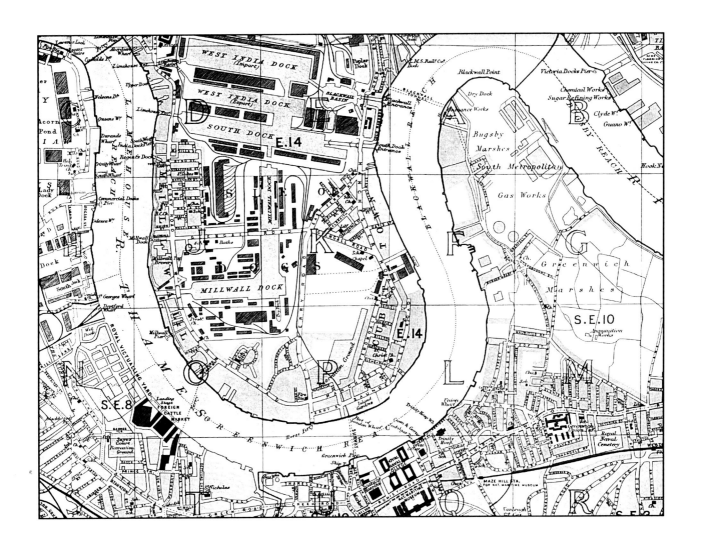

Map of the Isle of Dogs

c 1940

PART OF MY FAMILY TREE

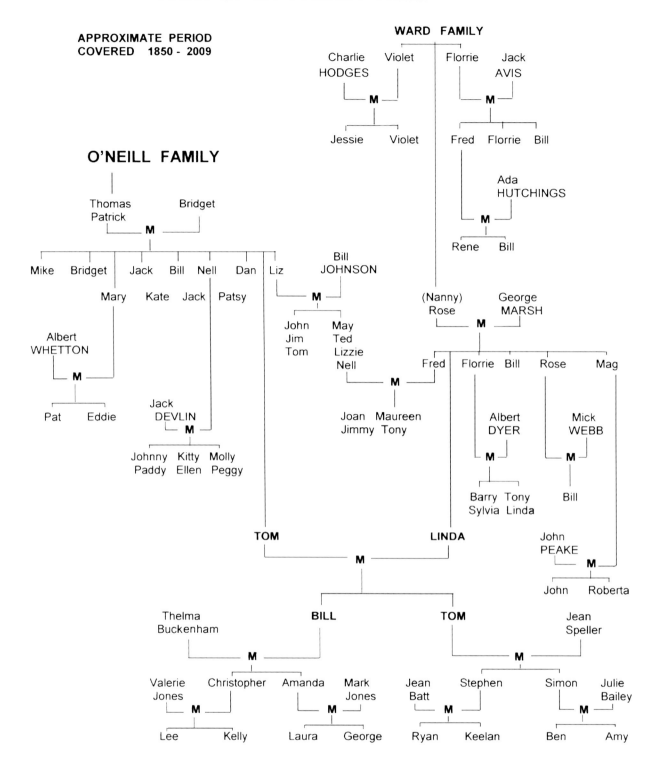

APPROXIMATE PERIOD COVERED 1850 - 2009

THIS PART OF MY FAMILY TREE SHOWS THE RELATIONSHIPS BETWEEN SOME OF OUR FAMILIES WHO LIVED ON THE ISLE OF DOGS AND WHO ARE REFERRED TO IN THIS BOOK

M denotes Married

1.1   MY FAMILY

I was born in the upstairs front room of 176 West Ferry Road, Millwall, London E14 on 21st October 1927 in the shadow of the Le-Bas Tube Company under the sign *'Cyclops Iron Works'* where my father worked for several years as a welder. My brother Tom was also born there on 17th July 1930. My Mother was born next door in No 178 West Ferry Road in December 1900 and my Father at 202 West Ferry Road in 1897.

I came from a very complicated family background mainly due to many couples meeting at various family weddings so a lot of my immediate relations were cousins, uncles and aunts at the same time and in consequence we used to have some large family parties. Just prior to the Second World War, there were over twenty closely related families living on the Island.

The main family names on my Father's side were *O'Neill, Johnson and Devlin* and on my Mother's side, *Marsh, Avis and Hodges*. Other connections through various marriages were *Hutchings, Dyer and Webb,* totalling approximately seventy five people. This, of course, was not unusual all over the country and it was the Second World War that split families up, in the East End of London in particular.

My Mother was the oldest of three sisters and two brothers. My Father was the youngest of six boys with five sisters of various ages.

All of the six boys served in the Great War, 1914-1918, and all came home safely, the only casualty being Uncle Jack who suffered all of his life with the effect of being gassed in the trenches.

My Dad served in the Royal Flying Corps where he first learnt the art of welding; in later years he was reckoned to be one of the top ten pipe welders in the country as reported in the trade magazine *'Ice Logic'*.

He once carried out a weld on ammonia pipes in the ducts under Cadby Hall, the Walls Ice Cream factory in London, working through three strategically placed mirrors. He was also involved in the pipework on the first ice skating rink in the Olympia, Kensington.

The family did not suffer any casualties during the 1939/45 War and to my knowledge there was only one fatal casualty during the First World War and that was Bill Avis, son of Jack and Flo Avis, Aunt Flo being my grandmother's sister. Bill was killed at Vimy Ridge July 1916 serving in the Royal West Kent Regiment.

Several of the family served in the armed forces during the Second World War including two WAAF's. The two that were mentioned in particular were Bill Dyer who served on HMS AJAX at the Battle of the River Plate and Johnny Devlin who served with distinction on HMS LONDON.

The Johnsons moved to Becontree in the early thirties and they were soon followed by their daughter Nell and her husband Fred, my Mother's brother, along with their two daughters, Joan and Maureen, with whom I am still in touch and see Joan quite regularly.

At the time of writing, 2008, I am one of if not the oldest of the family who lived in Millwall during the early thirties.

MAP of SOUTH WEST PART of THE ISLE OF DOGS

'MY PATCH' ON EITHER SIDE OF WEST FERRY ROAD

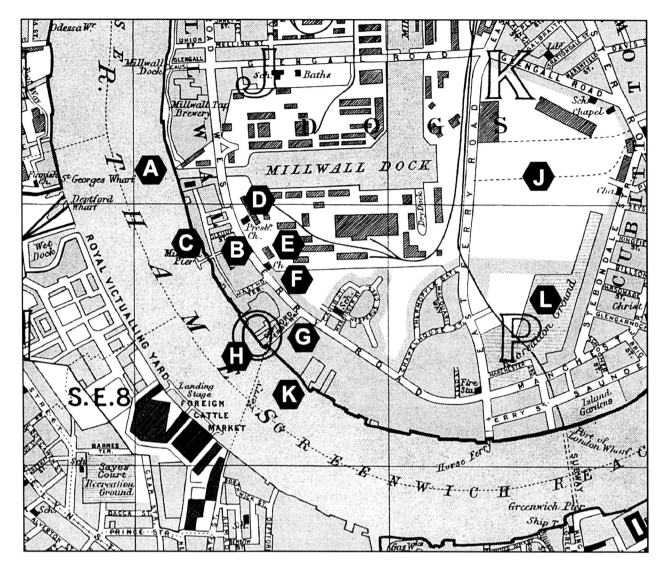

KEY			
A	Millwall Dock bridge which spanned the entrance to the docks	G	Until 1920 there was a small dairy farm here
B	176 West Ferry Road , where I was born	H	The ferry ceased to operate after the Greenwich tunnel was built
C	Le-Bas Tube Co. whose air raid shelters we used at nights and weekends	J	The Mudchute, now a town educational farm
D	St. Mildred's house and garden in St. Mildred's Square (behind the Scotch Church)	K	The launching site of the 'Great Eastern
E	St.Edmund's Roman Catholic Church	L	The New Park
F	St.Edmund's School where we were taught by L.C.C. (R.C.) teachers		

Before continuing with my memories of Millwall, I have included below a very short history of the area. This, together with the map opposite, will give you a better understanding of this part of the East End of London back in the 1920s and 1930s.

At the time that I was living there, 1927-1940, Millwall was in the Borough of Poplar. Now it is in the Borough of Tower Hamlets, the home of the *Canary Wharf* complex. It is situated on the west side of the Isle of Dogs, the area within the 'U' of the River Thames opposite Greenwich. At the beginning and end of each episode of *Eastenders* an aerial view clearly shows the location.

Millwall derives its name from the row of seven windmills that were built on a long wall along the western shoreline of the Island. They became a landmark to sailors sailing up river to London.

The Isle of Dogs is believed to have obtained its name in the days when the Kings and Queens of England had their Royal palace across the river at Greenwich and kept their hunting dogs on the Isle.

Until 1800 the Island was open countryside. In 1799 Parliament passed an Act allowing the building of docks on the Island. The West India Dock was the first to be built, followed by the Millwall Dock. Building the docks and bridges across the entrances to the docks from the river caused Millwall to really become an Island.

The docks attracted heavy industry and storage buildings soon arrived in the area with a leaning towards shipbuilding. By 1848 there were 38 firms on the Island and many of the roads and streets were named after land and factory owners.

Some world famous firms on the Island	
Mortons	Processed food and sweets
Brown and Lennox	Anchors and chains
Cutlers	Heavy engineering
Maconochies	Pan-Yan, tinned foods and famous for tinned rations for the troops in both world wars
Le-Bas Tubes	Pipe work
Westwoods	Gas holders and bridges
Matthew T. Shaw	Heavy steel fabrication
Yarrows	Small gun boats, moving north in 1906
Russells Yard	Built the Great Eastern, the largest ship of the 19th century
Manganese Bronze	Ships propellers
Hawkins and Timpsons	Rope manufacturers
Burrells	All types of marine paint etc.
Later McDougalls	Flour
Lenatons	Timber

The new complex of Canary Wharf was so named because it was built on the site of the old Canary Wharf where all of the ships unloaded their produce from the Canary Islands.

By 1970 the docks and the firms were history, due to the need for deep water terminals for today's container ships.

The Island had its own Football Club which started in 1885-86 season with a team from Mortons factory, *'Millwall Rovers'*. The club turned professional in 1883 and played at what is now Millwall Park or as I knew it the New Park, the Island Gardens Park being known as the Old Park. They often had crowds of 5,000 plus. In 1910 the club moved south of the river but to this day they are still known as *'Millwall Football Club'*.

1.2   GROWING UP IN MILLWALL

Growing up during the thirties on the Island was like living in a village, my immediate area was from the Millwall Dock bridge down to Cahir Street and later stretched around to the New Park and then the Old Park.

The *local* pubs from the bridge down were the *Kingsbridge*, the *Magnet and Dewdrop*, my Dad's pub, the *Ironmongers* and the *Vulcan. The Great Eastern* with the *Burns* and the *Ship* a bit further down, but the *Magnet and Dewdrop* was the family pub. I remember the licensees were Mr & Mrs Woodruffe.

I can remember some of my Dad's old mates like Old Trot, Fred Porter, Fred Blackabee, Bill Johnson , his brother-in-law and Diddy Williams. Diddy had a wooden leg and was the Island's *'knocker up'. This meant that he was paid *'tuppence'*, two old pennies, per week to wake people up for work. He would knock on the front door if his customers slept on the ground floor, and had a long pole with a piece of metal fixed to the end for those in the front first floor bedrooms. People got used to his timing by the bonk of his wooden leg on the pavement as he walked around. He lost a few customers because of it when, one Monday morning, he had a rubber pad put on his wooden leg and half of Millwall was late for work.

Some of the local shops I remember were Mrs Lewis' confectionery shop also selling toys and papers near the dock entrance. Jones' general stores was run by old Daddy Jones, his son Dave and sister Lil, who used to sing in the local concerts.

Next door to them was a sweet shop run by Ted Williams, then came Burgoyne's fruit shop. On the opposite side of the road, the river side and corner of Gaverick Street, was a café that sold treacle pudding in a basin. Witheys was a general store on the corner of Crewe Street and that was about it. For anything else you went over the bridge to Betz the butchers who made gorgeous faggots and pease pudding. Tom Baggs was the fishmonger and Joe Squires had a pawnshop.

In the other direction there was a new parade of shops at the Cahir Street flats.

Along by Nanny O'Neill, between the Magnet and the Ironmongers pubs was Wiggins the barbers, number 206, Bengivengo the cobblers and a small general store that sold sweets, bread, firewood and paraffin oil and hot sarsaparilla during the winter for ha'penny a glass, but it always smelt of paraffin.

On the opposite corner to the Ironmongers, across an opening known as the High Hill was another general store called Garetts. Opposite there, in front of Inglenheim Place was Mrs Roses and the Post Office, but these were pulled down when the Cahir Street flats were built during the early thirties.

Almost opposite my house and next door to Burgoyne's shop was the Convent. A bit further down past four terraced houses was St Edmund's Church and next to the Church St Edmund's School.

Behind the Convent and in Burgoyne's Square, where there was the lorry garage and lorry park, stood St Joseph's Hall.

The main factories in this area on the river side were Winkleys Oil Wharf and Snowdon Oil Wharf. Le-Bas Tube Ltd, Brown and Lennox and Cutlers. On the opposite side were the docks, McDougalls Flour Mill and Montague Myer Timber Yard.

West Ferry Road, looking north west towards St. Edmund's Church whose spire is just visible
I lived a bit further down the road, on the left.

View from the drawing room of St. Mildred's House, across West Ferry Road to Claude Street.
St. Paul's Presbyterian Church (The Scotch Church) on the right.
No 178 West Ferry Road was at the other end of the terraced row of houses on the left. The group
of women are looking at the wedding car in Claude Street. My mum was no doubt in the group.

(photographs - Island History Trust)

Millwall Dock
c 1919

Bridger at entrance to Millwall Dock
The pedestrian high level crossing can be clearly seen at the middle left

West India Dock
1949

BOW BELLS TO BOREHAMWOOD

The main traffic during the day was horse and cart and during the dinner hour there could be as many as a dozen horse and carts parked in the side streets.

One of our biggest problems was when ships and barges came into or out of Millwall Dock; the road and pedestrian bridge across the entrance would swing round stopping all traffic, sometimes for up to an hour. The only way across was by the lock gates, or the pedestrian bridge if only barges were going through. We called these *'bridgers'* and were used as an excuse for being late for school or work because the vast majority walked to work and school.

After 5.30 pm and at weekends only the occasional bus or car came along so we could play in the streets.

I remember the first bit of tarmacadam road that went down in Millwall was outside St Edmund's Catholic Church; we immediately turned it into our very own skating rink. This was my environment from 1927-1940.

I started school at St Edmund's when I was three years old, fell over during my first month there, broke my nose and did not go back until I was five.

(photograph - Island History Trust)

St. Edmund's School   1937
I am third from the right in the front row. Eileen Downey is third from the left in second row.
Lenny Bannister, my best mate at the time, is standing in front of Miss O'Connell on right

There were eight classrooms, six in the main building and two in the single storey annexe. There is no change in the school, but the church was demolished a few years ago and a new one built. I sent a contribution towards the cost of the new one in the family's name.

The Headmaster was Mr Robinson known as Beakey and the teachers whose classes I went through, from the bottom up, were Miss Mottram, Miss Pritchard, Miss O'Sullivan who was my favourite, Miss O'Connell, Miss Nolan, Miss Dennison, Mr O'Sullivan and Tommy Ryan. The caretaker was Mr Downey. My first schoolboy crush was on his niece, Eileen. I was in Mr Ryan's class when war broke out.

Mr O'Sullivan played cricket during holidays for Surrey; he used to get his batting practice in the playground at lunch times by putting a sixpenny piece on each of the stumps and get the older boys to bowl at him. A sixpence in those days was a King's ransom. I never did see anybody get a sixpence.

When I was seven I joined the cubs, meeting in St Joseph's Hall. The cubmaster was Billy Budd. A scout troop was formed by Mr Appleton who lived in Orpington. It was the *16th South Poplar Troop* and I was leader of *'Bulldog Patrol'*. I remember our first camp adventure was to Downe in Kent, we actually pulled a loaded trek cart from Millwall, through the Blackwall Tunnel to New Cross Station to save money. Fancy doing that now!

As we were late coming back on the holiday Monday evening we returned via Greenwich Tunnel. We unloaded and dismantled the trek cart to get it into the lift, assembled and loaded it at the bottom and repeated the operation at the other end. We arrived back at St Edmund's around midnight.

The other trips we did were a fortnight at Frylands Woods in Kent and in 1938 to Goring on Thames near Streatley, Berks. A few years ago I was near the site at Goring and found it quite easily, even the old boathouse was there, from which we borrowed a punt and did a trip up the river. I went to a tree and found my initials and date and to my knowledge they are still there.

I also belonged to the boxing club at St Joseph's and took part in one or two tournaments, one of them I remember was in the school playground.

'Smells good'
Scout camp. Goring-on-Thames
1939

Tom, Me and Billy Avis,
His nephew Ronnie in front c 1937

(All photos by the author Bill O'Neill)

The Greenwich Foot Tunnel was built in the late eighteen hundreds mainly to get workers from the Greenwich and Deptford areas to work in the London docks. The nearest bridge being Tower Bridge in the City and the only way to cross was by rowing boats and small ferry boats which during the winter months could not operate because of the fogs and heavy tides, the fogs lasting for days at a time.

In the middle of the two great domes is a huge round lift holding approximately 60 people and around it a large circular staircase with the tunnel being approximately a quarter of a mile long.

During the First World War my Mother, along with hundreds more, took shelter from the *'Zeppelin'* raids in the tunnel. It was not used as shelter during the Second World War as it was considered too dangerous. I would like as many pounds as the times I have walked or run through that tunnel. If you get a group of youngsters shouting the echo is deafening. On a busy day there would be a continuous line of people with large queues for the lifts at either end.

I remember my Dad telling me that he and all of his five brothers swam across the Thames from the *'Blackwall Rowing Club'* beach to the small beach in front of the Greenwich Naval College.

I became an altar boy at St Edmund's Church. The priest at the time was Father Melly and later Father Terry, the housekeeper being Miss Clements. Some of the sisters at the Convent I remember were Sister Josephine, Sister Mary and I think Sister Theresa. Being an altar boy meant being on duty several times a week, the average week being Benediction Friday evening, Confessional duty at least once a month, three Sunday morning Masses, Sunday evening Benediction, Wednesday early morning mass assisting the Sisters, plus all of the various Holy days

Brother Tom and I are in our 'Procession' suits.

Photo of Tom and me in our back 'garden' with our dog Prince - 176 West Ferry Road

(All photos by the author Bill O'Neill)

Every lunchtime between 12 and 12.30 we attended classes in the vestry for Latin pronunciation. I have often thought since that there would be six or seven young Cockney boys who would be learning Latin, who could not at times speak the King's English.

I was also a trainbearer to the May Queen, in the May procession that went all around the Island. The Queen of that year was a girl called Freeman, that was in about 1935. A few years later my younger brother Tom was cushion bearer in the same procession. Being a Catholic, attending St Edmund's School and becoming an altar boy, I took part in many of these processions.

May Queen Procession
I am the trainbearer on right

Mrs Devlin, Aunt Nell
by Nanny O'Neill's altar at
202 West Ferry Road in the 1920s

(photographs - Bill O'Neill)

I particularly remember the drum and fife bands and the many huge statues being carried around the Island by relays of men. Many of my uncles took part. I also remember having tea and buns in the school when we returned and then going out again in the evening as an altar boy to bless all of the altars built in the downstairs windows of the terraced houses and flats.

The whole window casements would be removed and a tiered stand stood in the window. White sheets would then be draped over the structure and the religious ornaments, pictures and candles would be displayed along with vases of flowers, usually lilies.

There would be approximately 10 – 12 altar boys ranging in age from eight years old to middle age, all dressed in black cassocks and white cotters. We would form a v on the pavement facing the altar, with the priest at the apex. The residents and their families would stand behind us with the neighbours behind them; the altar would then be blessed.

We would start about 7.00 pm and finish about 10.30 pm. We always went around the Island anti-clockwise so my Grandmother's altar at number 202 West Ferry Road was always the first to be blessed. Looking back I never ever remember it raining, but I do know that underneath nearly every altar was a crate or barrel of beer, if not both and true to the *Old East End* tradition when families met over a drink there were always a few differences of opinion.

In fact during the thirties one of the highlights for us kids was to look out of our bedroom windows on Saturday nights about 10.30 pm and watch the inevitable punch up as the pubs turned out. This also happened on some Sunday afternoons, because with large families and small houses there was no room to fight indoors.

Another East End tradition was to visit your grandparents on Sunday evenings. We all used to gather at Nanny O'Neill's when after a few drinks the six brothers, or how many were there, would nearly always get on to talking about the First World War. Cousins Ted, Jim and myself would sit as quiet as mice under the table listening to their stories of the trenches.

Mum
Billy Avis   Me
Brother Tom

(photograph - Bill O'Neill)

Another memory is of St Mildred's House. This was a large house set back from the main West Ferry Road opposite Claude Street just a few yards from No.176 where we lived. On one corner of St Mildred's Square was a row of terraced houses and on the other corner was the Scottish Presbyterian Church said to have been built by Scottish engineers brought down to work on the Island building the '*Great Eastern*' which was launched in 1858. The church known as St Paul's still stands today. St Mildred's House was a stand alone building, had seven bedrooms, a dining room, common room, kitchens and a chapel. There was also a large garden at the rear backing onto the docks and was later in the shadow of the McDougall flour mills.

The settlement was occupied by ladies of means, one of them we discovered many years later lived in Barnet Lane, Elstree and visited my mother when we lived in Boreham Wood. They were all addressed as *Miss* and did good work in the community by organising outings, visiting the sick, arranging various activities for mothers in particular. My mother along with many of the local mums belonged to the Friday Night Club. That was about the only outing some of them had. On the right hand side of St Mildred's House there was a large hall where concerts and jumble sales were held

As I am writing this other memories come flooding back like the bridgers and walking over the locks as I have already mentioned, delivering newspapers to the ships in Millwall Docks many of which had foreign crews who did not speak or understand the value of British coins, which enabled us to make a small '*profit*' from time to time when handing over change. Helping Uncle Jack Devlin on his cats'-meat rounds. He used to wear a large brown coat with a thick leather belt around his middle and over one shoulder to hold the large basket in which there were slices of horse meat on skewers. Nearly everybody on the Island had a cat to counter the mouse and rat population due mainly to the grain warehouses. I used to make sure that I served the three storey houses with basement '*aireys*' in Stebondale Street. I would throw an empty stick or two to the cat or cats in the airey, go up the steps to the front door and knock and when the occupant, usually a lady, answered the door I would point to the cat or cats licking the skewer and tell her the cats had eaten the meat. I would then be paid the one or two pence which enabled me to make up one or two more skewers of meat to sell. I did make sure that I did not do this to the same cats every time!

I think I remember telling all this to the priest when I went to confession!

Going up Glengall Causeway to see what we could scrounge off the barges at low tide and getting chased by the river police. Going to the Ideal Cinema in Poplar High Street and catching the number 56 bus back to Millwall. Going to the Old Queens Theatre to see a pantomime, going over to Deptford High Street on a Saturday evening to get the Sunday joint and leaving it as late as possible before buying to get the best price. Pressing your nose against the window of Nobles toy shop, pie and mash in '*Manzes*' while Dad had a pint in the 'White Swan' and then walking back through Greenwich Tunnel.

Greenwich Park on Sunday morning, or going to *Petticoat Lane* as special treat, not forgetting *Club Row* to look at the pups, kittens and birds.

Going to Southend on the *'Golden'* or *'Royal Eagle'* paddle steamers from Greenwich Pier. Shopping in Crisp Street and Watney Street Market, watching and listening to the *'Scotch Islanders Band'* who were a group of Islanders wearing highland dress including kilts.

The long hot summers during the school holidays spent mainly down the New Park with a bottle of cold tea and jam sandwiches. I wonder how many remember the ladder in the paddling pool and catching bloodsuckers in a jar.

Following the *'Frances and Walters'* horse drawn hearses with their purple plumes and livery.

The play centre at Harbinger School. *'Nitty Norah'* coming around the schools and the clinic where we used to go to have our cuts and bruises seen to, especially cut knees.

Going over the *'Mudchute'* to catch newts and frogs, standing in the crowd outside the front door of any house that had a wedding, funeral or an ambulance calling to take someone away.

The *'Mudchute'* was a very large mound covering some thirty acres formed by thousands of tons of silt pumped out to form the Millwall Docks and encased in banks of clinker during the late 1800s. Over the years the silty mud hardened and at the start of the First World War allotments were formed.

At the outbreak of the Second World War anti-aircraft gun batteries were built in the middle of the allotments and were in action throughout the War and broke many windows in the area in the process.

Today the Mudchute is a farm and stable complex open to the public and is also one of the stations on the *'Dockland Light Railway'*.

Other memories were of the games we used to play; they all had their seasons. There were the gutter marbles (or glarnies), whip and top, hoop and stick, roller skates and home made scooters. We used to roam the factories on the Island for ball bearings, which we used for wheels. I remember my brother, for one of his birthdays, having a proper scooter, I persuaded him to swap, he fell off and broke his leg. I got a good hiding and my mother spent six weeks pushing him through Greenwich Tunnel on a pram for treatment at the Seamen's Hospital in Greenwich.

Another sure clip around the ear would be if the kettle wasn't boiling, the bread not cut and the table not laid by exactly twenty to one for my mother and Aunt Florrie to rush home from Maconochies to get some lunch, or dinner as it was then known.

I have had to run many a time when the 12.30 whistle went and I was still playing on my way home from school.

During the 1938 crisis I was put down for *'evacuation'*. I had my case packed, my labels on and even got as far as assembling at St Edmund's School and if I remember rightly the buses were there waiting when news of Mr Chamberlain's visit to Munich came through. We all went home and those that had gone away came back. A lot of the children from Millwall went to the Abingdon and Somerset areas and from the tales that we heard from some of those who returned we didn't think that we had missed much.

There was no large river, no streets to play in and it was very dark at night.

During the next eight months or so things began to change. There were strange looking vehicles appearing; i.e. fire engines painted green, rescue service vehicles, ARP posts being built and set up, surface air raid shelters being built.

Little did I know that when I walked out of St Edmund's School late July 1939 at the start of the summer holiday it would be for the last time and also the last time I would see the majority of my school friends and classmates.

My world was about to change dramatically, also for many others, but many did not make it.

As children we respected our elders, especially our teachers and we were 'children' much longer in those days. If we deserved the cane we accepted it and parents did not rush down to the school and have a go at the teachers. We were in the main law abiding and the police used their common sense far more than they do now, and they seemed older. They knew their manors and a clip with their capes usually did the job. It was old fashioned community policing and the East End in particular had its own brand of discipline, which worked.

Just before the end of the 1939 summer term I sat an exam at the Cubitt Town School, that won me one of the three free places that were given to the Island schools to attend the George Green School in Poplar. I never set foot inside that school or in any other school in London, the reason being that at the outbreak of war in September many thousands of schoolchildren were evacuated and many of the schools were being turned into A.R.P. Fire and Rescue Service Centres; also many schools did not have adequate air raid shelters built in time.

The irony of that was that Dad had gone without a few pints and packets of fags to buy my uniform, etc.

I consider that although I left school at the age of twelve because of the War and did not do any serious schooling after, I received a very good basic education at St Edmund's and will always remember it as a very good school. I was always very happy there.

The names I can remember from my schooldays at St Edmund's are *Lenny Bannister*, my best mate, apart from my cousin *Billy Avis; Charlie Cash*, another good mate; *Japper Seymour; Terry Fitzgerald; Zippy Fry; Jimmy and Georgie Stone; Johnny and Harry Aldis; Martin Baggs; Johnnie and Eileen Downey* and her friend *Lily Knutsford; Nellie Barnett; Nellie Morgan; Wiggy Horton; Terry Goldring; Jean French* and *Tommy Taylor; Pat Kimberley* who lived in *Dunbar House, Glengall Road* was a senior scout in the troop with his elder brother *Bill*, a Rover Scout.

The family names I remember in the immediate vicinity were opposite: *Horton, Hale, Goldring* and *Porter*, next door at number 174, downstairs, *Mr Bullock* and his *daughter*, with her daughter *Ivy*, upstairs were the *Landers*, with daughter *Edith* and son *Freddie*; next door to them the *Noolans*, one of their sons, *Wally*, was one of my mates. Next to them upstairs lived *Ronnie Martin*, another of my mates and downstairs the *Taylors*; their daughter *Rose* was about my age and one of her best friends was *Elsie Waters* who lived with her parents and elder sister at number 180 West Ferry Road. *Elsie* went to the Millwall Secondary School in Janet Street and one of her best friends at school was *Frances Tyler* who married *Ernie Jones* of Thermopylae Gate, now one of my best friends. Family friends were the *Claydons* and *Stones* from Claude Street.

Another part of life on the Island in the thirties was the pawnshop. Our local one was *Joe Squires* over the bridge, opposite Janet Street.

The amazing thing here was that the people taking things to pawn on a Monday morning would not take them into the pawnshop themselves but take them, or send their children with them, to a pawnshop lady who did it for them.

The two I remember were *Jessie Pye*, who lived in Claude Street and my *Aunt Violet Hodges*, who lived next door to Squires pawnshop. They both had forms in their front rooms which were used as waiting rooms.

Aunt Jessie had an old piano in her front room and all of the children used to play *chopsticks* on it; this became known as the pawnshop tune within the family. I can still see *Jessie Pye* now in her sack apron and man's cap pushing her pram with all of the parcels on. Monday they went in and Fridays they came out.

Another character lived next door but one to the Magnet pub. *Jess Elms, Aunt Jessie* as we knew her, was a very large lady with a heart of gold; she always sat outside on her front room window ledge.

Living between her and the Magnet was *Bob Roberts*, the fish and winkle man, coming around the Island every Sunday selling his brown bags of winkles from his barrow. I earned many a penny in his back yard shed washing his pans out.

Public houses were an important part of life in the East End before the War, very few women used them. When they did it was mainly at week-ends, Sunday evenings in particular and at family gatherings and usually in the *posh* private bar. The pubs that I remember that were in the area of the map of the South West part of the Island were as follows:

- The Blacksmith
- The North Pole
- The Pin and Cotter
- The Tooke Arms
- The Dock House
- The Kingsbridge
- The Magnet and Dewdrop
- The Ironmongers
- The Vulcan
- The Great Eastern
- The Robbie Burns
- The Manchester Arms
- The Ferry House
- The Waterman's Arms
- The Devonshire Arms.

Joe Squires' pawnshop in West Ferry Road. My aunt Jessie Hodges and family lived next door on the ground-floor. Fred Marsh and family, who moved to Becontree in 1933, lived on the floor above

(photograph - Island History Trust)

In those days pub landlords were treated like *'Lords of the Manor'* and were always referred to as the *guv'nor* as was his missus. You always wore your best suit fresh from the pawnshop to go to the pub on Sundays. The *guv'nor* would usually be dressed up and sit with his customers and more often than not there would be snacks on the bar.

Opening hours were very short. On Sundays it was 12 – 2pm and 7 – 10pm and on both sessions there would be a crowd of men standing talking after *'chucking out'* sometimes for up to an hour. This practice slowly disappeared in the early fifties.

Most of them were *'family pubs'*; by that I mean they were used by quite a few generations over a period. Once *'it'* became your pub very rarely would you change it, sometimes passing two or three other pubs to visit yours.

They were the meeting places for births, deaths and marriages and any other family gathering. Every pub had a piano. Very few punch ups occurred in the pub, always outside in the street, usually it would be one to one with a ring of onlookers formed around them and to see fair play. Once you were knocked down then that was it, no kicking or knives, unlike today. The police always patrolled in pairs; they were always six foot tall and they often turned a blind eye to pub fights knowing that the participants would be friends the next day. If family members were involved as was often the case the family would turn on the police, so again common sense was applied.

During the thirties the game of darts became very popular; the early darts boards were made of elm and needed soaking when not in use and were called *'five-ten boards'* i.e. only having 5, 10, 15, 20 segments three times around the board. Some had no treble section. The 20 sections were one being where it is now and roughly where 10 and 16 are on the modern clock boards.

London Fives or Five-Tens Dartboard

Bookmakers operated from houses and were continually raided by police and I earned many a threepenny bit by acting as lookout. Near neighbours kept their front and back doors unlocked so that the bookmakers and their customers could escape through houses and over garden walls when raided. Those that were caught were taken in a *Black Maria* police van to the police station and were let out on bail on receipt of ten shillings (50p) and proof of who they were by showing a rent book. They appeared at Arbour Square Magistrates Court and were fined accordingly.

Children were very often used to take betting slips to the bookmaker's house.

Among the regular customers at the police station were my Dad and Uncle Jack Avis.

In those days people did not travel too far from home and Poplar was the farthest some travelled with months in between trips; very, very few had cars. I can only remember one member of the whole family who owned a car before the War and that was *Albert Dyer*. We as kids spent more time pushing it to start than he did driving it.

I was about eight or nine before I had my first ride in a car. Dad and Uncle Jack Avis hired a friend's car to take us all to Chatham Navy Week for a day. Four adults, three children and the driver. I have never forgotten that trip going over Tower Bridge and coming back through

Rotherhithe Tunnel at night, I even remember the driver's name, '*Alf*!'

The next car I rode in was Bill Munt's a few years later in Boreham Wood about 1942. A ride on a tram was always an adventure. The nearest trams to us terminated at the entrance to the West India Docks outside the pub called the *Blue Post* opposite *Charlie Brown's* pub; they were very noisy and swayed about a lot. The tram lines were in the middle of the road and when getting off you had to be careful that you did not get run over by the traffic coming past you between the tram and the kerb. Our other tram ride used to be between Greenwich and Deptford; nearly all the time they were moving the driver would ring a bell. Many a bicycle would catch their wheels in the tram lines. The old joke was that you had to push your bike to the depot to get it out.

One of our biggest Bank Holiday treats was to go to the very large fairground on Blackheath, that is if we could get Dad to come out of the Magnet and Dewdrop sober on the Bank Holiday Monday lunchtime. We did make it a few times. We would trudge back through Greenwich Tunnel clutching our coconuts, wearing our jockey caps plus anything else we had picked up, usually about 8.00 pm, and Dad would then return to the Magnet and pick up where he had left off.

I am not suggesting that he was a '*boozer*' as such, he just liked his pint or three of Mann & Crossmans beer.

I suppose on reflection in those days they worked long hard hours and it was the only real relaxation they had, but then this also applied to the women, but by and large they had to put up with it.

The women were the real backbone of the East End of London and most families had a patriarch of a grandmother; I know I did in the form of Nanny Marsh. I have seen her face up to a man in the street when defending one of her brood and winning.

Nanny O'Neill was totally different, never ever going out, always dressed in black, sitting in her armchair by the fire quite content with her half ounce of Wilson's snuff. I remember her saying to my Dad, "*Those sardines make me feel sick*'" He replied, "*Well, don't eat them then.*" She answered back, "*No, not them sardines, those that go off when Hitler's coming.*" She of course meant sirens. She had several grandchildren and never could remember all of our names. She died in Becontree not long after we had moved to Boreham Wood in 1941.

Another one of our treats in the school holidays was to go over to Greenwich and sit on the *beach* in front of the palace at low tide. It was about four or five yards wide and a couple of hundred yards long and used to get quite crowded. For a penny you could get a trip along the river in a rowing boat but you needed a bath when you got home if you had been in for a swim!

It was from Greenwich that I saw the German cruise liner '*Monte Rosa*' sailing up to the Pool of London. It was captured at the end of the War and re-named '*The Empire Windrush*' and used as a troopship. In 1946 I missed sailing on her by twenty-four hours due to signal failure on the London to Harwich line. It was later used to bring immigrants over from the West Indies. It caught fire and sank in 1954.

It was suggested after the War that '*Luftwaffe*' pilots and navigators often sailed on the *Monte Rosa* when she visited London to take notes etc. on the docks, their approaches and layouts – I wonder?

So all in all life on Millwall was not all bad and I suppose not knowing any different helped.

1.3   HOP PICKING IN KENT

Hop picking or *'hopping'* was the *'Londoner's holiday'*. Hop pickers came mainly from the East End and areas of South East London. Up to about the mid-seventies all hops were hand-picked. The vast majority of hop fields were in Kent. Hops are not only used for brewing as they have many other uses.

It was quite hard work and to make your money you needed to put the hours in, usually a forty four hour week.

One of my first memories of hopping was when I was about five years old, we were on a farm in Hunton Bridge, Kent with my Father's sister – Aunt Liz Johnson and her family when somehow or other a polepuller's hook caught my right temple and blood spurted out like a fountain! Aunty Liz took off her apron and wrapped it around my head and along with my Mother we started to walk to Hunton Common where there was a first aid caravan set up to serve the surrounding hop fields. On the way we met the local policeman on his bicycle who produced a bandage and bandaged my head.

On reaching the caravan I remember kneeling in front of the doctor while the nurse removed the bandage and when they had cleaned me up and the bleeding had stopped, all there was to show was a pin-prick in my temple, so I expect that was the first of my nine lives – I can still remember the incident in great detail.

A *'polepuller's hook'* was a very sharp curved knife going to a very sharp point which they used to cut down the hop bines to allow them to fall over the hop bins ready for the hops to be picked.

Apart from going to Hunton Bridge we went to Yalding, Paddock Wood and Tonbridge. We usually went with my Mother's mother – Nanny Marsh but I must say that my Mum was never really keen on hopping, a bit too rough and ready, but as kids we loved it. London families usually went to the same farm year after year and it was Paddock Wood where we went between 1935-1939, always to the same hut on the same farm, in fact Nanny Marsh had an old iron bedstead in her hut and some even papered them out. The huts were brick-built, with a corrugated iron roof, a door and ventilation slats above which some had glass and a concrete floor approximately three metres wide and four metres deep. Lighting was by oil lamps. The huts were normally in a block of six with the covered cooking area in the middle of the block. An 'A' frame stood over a wood fire from which you hung your pots and the fire was contained in a two brick high oblong with a few bricks inside it to take frying pans for fry-ups.

The farmer would supply bundles of *'faggot's* for firewood. Faggots were usually brushwood and tree and hedge clippings which had been stored and dried out for that purpose so stew, usually rabbit, was nearly always on the menu. The cooking smells added to that of the firewood to us townies was like living in another world.

The beds were made up from straw and hay provided by the farmer, along with the mattress covers, usually sacking so you took all of your own top bedding, mats and chairs. The toilet facilities were very basic – then they were at home anyway. Water was supplied from a stand-pipe.

The procedure for going hopping was as follows…... About January you would write to the farm in question and book your hut, or huts, and around June or July you received your letter confirming your booking. From the first of June onwards Nanny Marsh would be on her doorstep waiting for the postman.

View of a Hopfield with
Oast House, used for
drying hops, in the
background
Paddock Wood - 1935

Part of a 1930s map
of Kent
The dotted line enclosed
area includes the hop
picking locations favoured
by the O'Neill family.

Me aged 7, standing
outside of one of the
huts.
The cooking area
is between the two huts.
Paddock Wood - 1935

(photographs - Bill O'Neill)

One year the family hid her letter but let her know that those around her had received theirs, the language when she found out was pure East-End. She was a tough old Cockney grandmother! The letter also confirmed your arrival date to coincide with the hop crop, usually between the last weeks in August to the first week in September for a period of 4-6 weeks again depending on the hop crop. So the whole of August was spent packing the boxes and bags that we would be taking.

We usually went down to Kent on the back of a lorry, but if there was not room for all after all of the goods and chattels had been loaded then some would go over to London Bridge Station to go by train, usually a late one which was called the *'Hopping Special'* and was a bit cheaper. Some of the smaller children were put up on the luggage rack until the ticket inspector had been round!

I remember on one occasion I was up on one rack and my cousin Billy Avis on the other, when the ticket inspector came round and Billy being a bit younger and more nervous pee'd himself which came down from the rack and over his mother and one of his aunts sitting below. I can't quite recall the outcome though.

Work began in the fields at 7.30 am, 12-1 pm for a lunch break then back again until 4.30 pm with half day on a Saturday. If the hop field you were working on was more than two fields away, transport was provided by the farmer, usually a flat top cart pulled by horses or a tractor. If you were late, you walked!

Everyday various food suppliers visited the hop fields with vans and trade bikes and we always had the *lolly man* come round too with his familiar cry of *"Cry baby cry, make your Mummy buy, lolly, lolly, lolly"*. They were ice lollies on sticks, all colours.

Even in hot weather it was always very cool in the hop fields. We worked under a canopy of hops strung over wires between the hop poles. Hops grew on clay soil so if there was rain the fields got very heavy with mud but it never seemed to rain while we were *'down hopping'*!

The bins were made of sacking stretched between two wooden folding frames with handles protruding at each end to allow you to move the bin along the row of hops. About 4.15 pm, the cry would go up *"Pull no more bines"* and this was so that the last tally of the day could be taken before packing up for the day. The tally man and his assistants would visit each bin three to four times per day to measure out the hops from the bins and put them in large sacks called *'pokes'* and would mark your tally book accordingly. There would usually be 2-4 people working one bin.

Every morning and afternoon, I would have to clean pick two upside down umbrellas full of hops before I could go and play. Clean picking meant no bine pieces or leaves. This was also the case with the bins. Once released I would go on the scrounge along with a mate or two. Our first priority, without getting caught, would be to visit the various fields and *borrow* potatoes, cabbages, turnips, swedes, *'hopping apples'* (those very big green ones), Victoria plums and pears plus anything else in season. We would then put them in sacks and hide them until early evening when they would then go in the pot. Of course we would sell some to other pickers. Through one of the village boys we soon learnt the art of ferreting and would give him a penny for the loan of his ferret plus a ha'penny for every rabbit caught – Nanny Marsh was a dab hand at skinning a rabbit! We even tried trout fishing but made too much noise and got caught and we were chased off.

Kent was not known as the *'Garden of England'* for nothing and some of those lads going hopping for the first time were amazed that vegetables and fruit did not grow on barrows in street markets.

Hop picking at Paddock Wood

Hop Picking Group

| ? | Mrs Leslie | Walter Leslie | Nellie Heron | Mum (Linda) |

Nellie's Daughter   Nanny Marsh

(photographs - Bill O'Neill)

On Friday night the dads, brothers and sisters who were working would arrive and stay until Sunday evening so the local pubs did a very good trade. The pubs that I remember were the *Railway Tavern,* Paddock Wood and the *Woolpack* at Yalding. The pubs charged a one shilling deposit on glasses so we lads were always on the look out for unattended glasses. A shilling in those days being a King's ransom.

Saturday nights usually finished up with a sing-song around the camp fire, the jug and glass doing the rounds and with someone always managing some sandwiches. More often than not, there would be a piano accordion or squeeze-box and sometimes a wind up gramophone was produced.

Hop picking was the *'Eastenders'* holiday but also very hard work. After a day or two your fingers would be black from the hops and it would take a week or two to wear off when you returned home. The pay was very minimal and averaged about three pounds per week per person working a 45 hour week payable at the end of the season. Those that had no husband visiting week-ends usually had to sub from the farmer to get by, in fact most people did and by the time they had paid for their transport etc. they were lucky to finish up with a tenner, but at least they had a holiday!

Whenever I am in Kent or Sussex during September, I always try to get hold of some hops, crush them between my fingers and smell them. The memories come flooding back.

The last time I was on a working hopfield was in 1946 when on leave from the R.A.F. and spent a week-end at Paddock Wood along with my cousin Billy Avis and Bluey Wilkinson both on leave from the Army. Nanny Marsh and Aunt Rose Webb both had bins and when we all went to pick at Rose's bin the language from Nanny Marsh made the hops blush.

Hop Pickers Meal Time - c 1933

Aunt Liz Johnson   Mary Johnson Teddy Johnson ?   Bet Johnson   Linda O'Neill   Bill O'Neill

Outside St. Mildred's School

Children carrying their gas masks on the way home.
In the background just left of centre,
I'm waiting to collect my
brother Tom
c 1939

More children from the school
making their way home.

Outside the brick-built air raid
shelters in St Mildred's Square.

A group of dockside buildings
close to home

(photographs - Bill O'Neill)

Back yard of 176 West Ferry Road
mid 1930s

Probably King George V Jubilee
Included are Young Florrie Avis,
Bill, Aunt Rose, Aunt Flo Dyer (who
moved to Boreham Wood 1938) and
Nanny Marsh

Left. Helping the gardener at
St Mildred's House 1935.

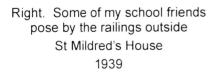

Right. Some of my school friends
pose by the railings outside
St Mildred's House
1939

1.4   THE FIRST YEAR OF WORLD WAR TWO

Came the 1939 crisis and war was declared. At that time Mother, my brother and myself were on holiday in a village called Wouldham, near Rochester in Kent with my Aunty Holly and Uncle Henry Martin (no relation but very old friends of my Mother), with Dad coming down at weekends. While there we were taken daily by lorry to the local hop fields leaving at 7.30 am and arriving back in Wouldham about 5.00 pm.

After a few weeks nothing seemed to be happening, so along with many others, especially those who stayed on in the Kent hop fields, we all began to drift back to the Island where we were kept busy filling sandbags for the Anderson air raid shelters we were all putting in our small back gardens.

All of the factories and docks were very busy. It was a different Millwall, now especially with the black-out in operation.

All of the schools were taken over by the various civil defence forces so our schooling was down to two or three mornings a week in St Mildred's House, so for the first time I was going to school with my *'Proddie'* mates. *Proddie* was the slang word for Protestants i.e. Church of England, and most of my friends and some of my relations went to *British Street School*. I had a foot in both camps.

One of the more upsetting things caused by the declaration of war was when the Government encouraged people to have their pets put to sleep, dogs in particular. We at the time had a small black Pomeranian named Prince; I can still remember Dad taking him to a unit set up in the playground of Harbinger School where no charge was made. As it happened, with the *Blitz* to come, it was probably the kindest thing to do.

As boys, our new headquarters was the surface air raid shelter in St Mildred's Square and we defended it from gangs from over the bridge and the *'Hesperus Crescent Gangs'* usually led by *Dodger Porter.* We used to have some right old stone throwing battles until a window was broken, when within seconds there was not a soul to be seen.

And so the summer of 1940 approached, which brought *'Dunkirk'.* I remember going up to the pier head, that was over the bridge and turn left before the donkey field opposite the Seamen's Mission and the Dock House, to see the flotillas of small boats going down the Thames to Dunkirk. We really did not know what it was all about but understood a bit more when they were coming back, especially when some of the larger craft had wounded on board and soldiers lining their decks.

We even had one or two warships come into the docks for repair. I think I can remember *HMS Cossack* from *Narvik* fame coming in for repair; perhaps somebody could confirm this.

There came the *'Battle of Britain'* and what an adventure that was for us young lads, watching the vapour trails and quickly becoming very expert in aircraft recognition, including engine sounds. Even now, nearly seventy years later, I can instantly recognise the sound of a *'Spitfire'.* We also became expert in recognising the sound of the German aircraft. We spent most of the time in these early days running in and out of the shelters.

I remember Florrie Avis getting married during August 1940 in the Scotch church opposite to where we lived. The service was interrupted at least three times.

We used to use our *'Anderson Shelters'* during the day and several of the local families used to use the *Le-Bas Tube shelters* at night.

We had several noisy nights mainly from anti-aircraft fire. Collecting shrapnel became our daytime hobby. To us boys we now had new heroes to replace the Hollywood cowboys. The first of the few fighter pilots, *Douglas Bader, Sailor Malan, Paddy Finucane, Johnny Johnson, Ginger Lacy* and many more.

Came the big one on that fateful Saturday afternoon in September. I remember I was out with the scout troop collecting waste paper in the trek cart. The sirens went yet again; we were just coming over Millwall Dock Bridge on our way back to St Joseph's Hall to unload when we realised that this time it was for real. My lasting memory was that of the *'Stuka'* dive bombers and the screaming noise they made. I remember thinking that if I had been taller I could have grabbed the wheels of their undercarriage.

The scoutmaster, Mr Appleton, told us to run for it. We dumped the loaded trek cart outside St Joseph's Hall and then ran for home, mine being the nearest by far. The sky above seemed to be filled with aircraft, mostly twin-engined bombers and I could clearly see the black cross on their wings. There seemed to be two layers, the high layer in formation with individual aircraft flying below them, no doubt the ones dropping the bombs.

The noise was deafening with the Mudchute anti-aircraft guns going full out. The fires had not yet started in earnest but there was plenty of smoke and dust.

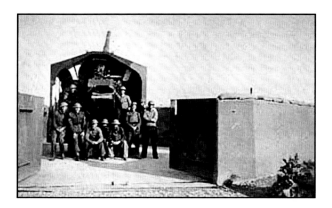

Mudchute anti-Aircraft Gun

Early in 1939 we had moved from upstairs in 176 to downstairs in 178. Nan and Grandad Marsh moved upstairs after Flo and Albert Dyer moved to Elstree, so I made for the shelter in the back garden of 178 where the rest of the family were. As I jumped in Dad gave me a clip for worrying Mother for not being in the shelter before the bombs fell. Those few minutes before I dived into the air raid shelter seemed like a lifetime.

The raid started at about 4.45 pm and finished about 6.00 pm and Millwall was alight, there was no gas, electricity or water but in true East End tradition a way was found to make a cup of tea.

A stand pipe soon produced water and the local ladies queued for my Dad to boil their kettles using his welding torch.

A very true and amusing story comes from this, my Mother queued for her turn and when her kettle boiled she took it into the living room and poured the boiling water around the cracks in the hearth because she heard a cricket down there and they were considered to be unlucky indoors. I can't remember if my Dad swore or not!

By now the Isle of Dogs was cut off from the rest of London, both bridges being put out of action and the whole of *'Docklands'* seemed to be on fire.

The raiders returned about 8.00 pm and left early next morning.

I remember coming out of *Le-Bas* gates and being amazed to see our houses still standing.

The tip of the starboard wing of the Heinkell 111 bomber is above our house in West Ferry Road

St Cuthbert's Church
After the bombing on 7/8 September 1940
The damaged building in the background is Harbinger School

(photograph - Island History Trust)

I also vividly remember walking down to see the remains of St Cuthbert's Church.

For that first four days and nights of the *Blitz* we were constantly taking cover; the whole of the docks were ablaze with barrels of oil exploding on the oil wharfs. My Dad and several of his work mates and neighbours spent many hours at high tide pushing burning barges away from the Le-Bas Tube Wharf which had so far escaped the fires. The other problem was the large rats that were everywhere, escaping from the grain stores that served McDougalls Flour Company. For the first twenty four hours there was no mains water, gas or electricity on the Island. Standpipes were soon put up and there were plenty of fires to boil a kettle on!

In between the raids unexploded bombs were going off which slowed up rescue and fire fighting work. Looking back I don't understand why more time bombs were not used, they caused more problems by disrupting everything in the area. One '*H.E. bomb*' could damage a part of a factory but one '*U.X.B.*' closed the whole factory down, sometimes for a few days.

I remember vividly on the Sunday evening before the sirens went, taking a flask of tea up to Dad at the wharf's edge where they were watching the tide, and seeing London alight. The Surrey Commercial docks almost opposite Millwall had dozens of barges full of pit props which were on fire and floating out and going down river on the tide. Looking up river it was a sight I shall never forget, the heat and the acrid smell of burning oil made your eyes water. The river was full of smoking and burning bits and pieces.

During the raids the noise was horrendous with the anti-aircraft gunfire. The sound of the bombs coming down, some with their tail fins modified to create a screaming noise, the near bomb explosions that made the shelter shake with dust etc. continually falling. Sometimes the lights went out and shock waves from near misses coming through the shelter plus the constant droning of the German aircraft overhead.

Aunt Rose Webb along with her husband Mike and his family were in a surface air raid shelter in Samuda Street when the row of terrace houses of which one of them was theirs were destroyed by an aerial torpedo. The lights in the shelter went out and most of the occupants were knocked to the floor by the blast wave. In the silence that always seems to follow these incidents Rose started calling for Mike, saying that the roof had collapsed and she was trapped. When the lighting had been restored they found that she had rolled under the bench seating!

I have often wished that I had at the time one of today's video cameras, not only would the film be priceless but I could convince myself that it did really happen.

Our Bomb

A small shrapnel bomb fell literally on our doorstep, at the time we were in the air raid shelter of the Le-Bas Tube Co. along with all of our immediate neighbours. Although the row of terraced houses (No 178 being on one end) did not collapse, most of the internal walls and doors were wrecked with very little recoverable. Dad then decided that enough was enough so he somehow got hold of an open back lorry and driver from Le-Bas, loaded what family we could get on board with what we could salvage and carry and set off for our relations in Becontree.

There were thirteen of us on board. Aunt Florrie and Uncle Jack Avis along with son Bill, their daughter Flo and her husband Harry Hatt were dropped off at friends in Gorsebrook Road, Dagenham. There was also Dad's sister Aunt Bridge, her husband Frank Page along with Paddy Devlin who they had taken in when his mother, Aunt Nell Devlin who was another of Dad's sisters who died when Paddy was a few months old. They stayed in Babington Road with Mum's brother Uncle Fred Marsh and his family.

Nanny O'Neill, who was nearly ninety years old, along with our family stayed with Aunt Liz who was another of Dad's sisters and Uncle Bill Johnson's family in Marlborough Road, plus their family so the Anderson air raid shelter was pretty crowded at times, but it was our bedroom for seven months.

I don't remember what we had to eat over that week-end, we must have had something but what I do remember vividly is the six hour journey of approximately twelve miles on the back of the lorry from Millwall to Becontree, the driver having to change his route several times due to fires and bomb craters plus the two air raid warnings.

We reached *No 104 Marlborough Road* about 6 pm. Aunt Liz had a large saucepan of soup on her kitchen range and I can still remember the smell and taste of that soup as we tucked in with plenty of crusty bread. It was like manna from heaven.

Scarcely had we finished eating when the air raid sirens went for the evening raid. We just about made it to the shelter before the first bombs fell. We were all totally exhausted and the bombs were not quite so close as on Millwall. I do remember sleeping the whole night through for the first time since the *Blitz* started.

I then began exploring my new surroundings

How our other family members fared in the *Blitz*

Over the next few months meeting other members of the family who had lived on Millwall we learnt a bit more of what they had experienced during the early days of the *Blitz*. Eileen Devlin, one of my cousins, lived on the top floor of a block of flats in Glengall Road that received a direct hit on the Saturday afternoon causing it to collapse. She was in the kitchen at the time and survived.

Fred Avis, Aunt Florrie's son, was at the time working at a brewery delivery company and they were held up at an incident where they were trying to reach someone buried in a collapsed house. Fred was tall and slim and the rescuers asked him to wriggle through a hole they had dug in the rubble. He reached the kitchen area and saw a woman lying on her back with her head towards him. He could just reach her head and pulled; her head came off in his hands. He was off work for sometime and never quite the same afterwards.

Uncle George Marsh was caught in a raid on his way home and dived into a surface communal air raid shelter. During a lull in the raid he decided to make a run for it; within seconds the shelter was hit by an unexploded anti-aircraft shell resulting in heavy casualties. Damage caused by unexploded anti-aircraft shells during the *Blitz* was quite a common occurrence.

Harry Hatt who married young Florrie Avis a week or two before the *Blitz* started had a motorbike and sidecar. After moving to Becontree he returned to the Island to pick up his bike and sidecar. On his way back coming through Canning Town he was blown off his bike by an unexploded bomb; the bike carried on and went down the hole caused by the bomb. Luckily he had a helmet, goggles and a heavy coat on. He was deaf for several weeks afterwards. He was taken back to Becontree by one of the rescue trucks. We had quite a laugh when Florrie told us what he looked like when she opened the door to him. A black face with two large white eyes where his goggles had been, his leather jacket covered in small holes and one shoe missing. He was only five feet tall and a bit rotund. He joined the '*Home Guard*' and when he had his greatcoat and helmet on you could hardly see him. The Avis family were allocated a house in Oval Road North in Dagenham. It looked out over Hornchurch Aerodrome and we spent hours watching the Spitfires coming and going and cheering when they did a victory roll.

Aunt Bridget and Co. were later housed in Babington Road almost opposite Uncle Fred Marsh where they had been staying. As I have already mentioned after seven months we were housed in Ilford. So all in all a bit of shrapnel in Mum's bum, two dead budgies and one lost dog; as a family we did not do too badly. It could have been far worse. Nanny O'Neill died while staying in Marlborough Road.

MAP SHOWING THE PART OF

BECONTREE WHERE I LIVED

1940 to 1941

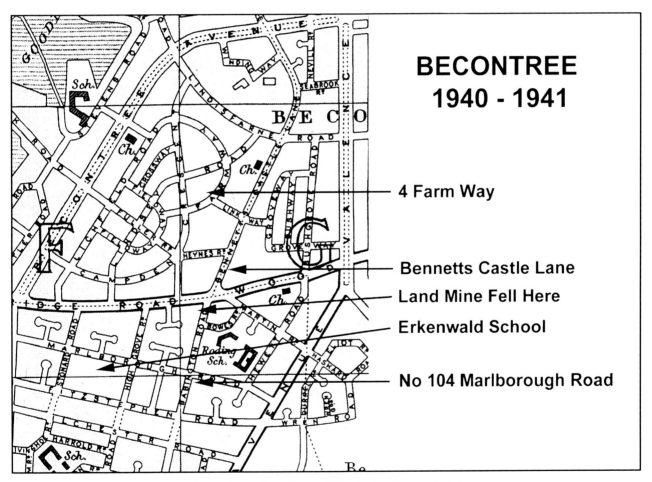

The area as shown has altered very little during the past sixty years or so.

1.5 BECONTREE

Becontree is a large town in Essex that was created by the London County Council between the wars (WW1 and WW11) to provide subsidised housing for the ever-expanding population of London. Covering approximately four square miles it is located between Chadwell Heath in the North and the River Thames in the South.

The main industries at the time, apart from the London docks, were the Ford Motor Company, Briggs Car Bodies, many car component subsidiaries, May and Bakers and towards Ilford Plesseys.

During the War Barking Park had a large anti-aircraft gun battery, Hornchurch was a Battle of Britain RAF fighter station. Most of the unexploded bombs dropped on London were detonated on the Rainham Marshes.

It was very different from living on Millwall. All of the houses had front and back gardens, inside toilets and bathrooms and no families shared a house; that is until the *Blitz* started.

This phase of the *Blitz* lasted for seven months. Records show that during this period there were very few nights when no bombing raids by the Germans took place, the usual alert period being from approximately 6.30 pm until 5 am. It was an experience you never ever really forget, living through over two hundred air raids and Dagenham and Becontree being on the route to the London docks in particular. Bombs were dropped locally at regular intervals, but at least we did not have the fires to cope with as we did on Millwall.

Although our address was 104 Marlborough Road, Becontree the only bedroom we had was the Anderson shelter in the garden which was virtually our home for the next seven months.

I don't remember being frightened or terrified as such at the start of the *Blitz*, it just suddenly happened and it seemed like a big adventure and quite unreal. It seemed as though it could all stop as suddenly as it began, but as time went on it just took over from ordinary everyday life, as we had known it. On occasions the nightly raids were later than usual and you would lie in the shelter, ears straining, hoping not to hear the air raid sirens in the distance and feeling relieved in a funny sort of way when you did. Then, as they got nearer and louder, you knew Jerry was on his way again. There would then be an eerie silence, sometimes for only minutes, other times for half an hour or so, then you would hear the distant sound of the anti-aircraft guns slowly getting louder as the local guns took over, then the sound of the German bombers, their engines always slightly out of synchronisation so giving a double *'buzz'*. You could tell the difference between the various types of anti-aircraft guns, the more rapid fire of the Bofors and the *'crack'* of some of the mobile guns, which sometimes broke more windows than the bombs did.

You heard some bombs coming by their whistle, which was followed by a rush of air and a deep thud that shook the shelter. You could also pick out the unexploded bombs by the different noise on impact. A near miss would be followed by falling debris, whistles blowing and fire and rescue services arriving at the scene, sometimes only a few doors or streets away.

As the wave of bombers passed anti-aircraft fire would be sporadic until the next wave; then it would begin all over again. By now realising what it was all about your stomach would knot up at the sound of the air raid warning and the all clear siren was music to your ears. Even now whenever I hear an air raid siren the hairs on the back of my neck stand up.

After every raid we would go out collecting shrapnel on the paths and roads and in people's front gardens. Shrapnel were mainly anti-aircraft shell fragments with the odd nose cone and base plate.

Prize finds were incendiary bomb tail fins, pieces of bomb or land mine, land mine parachute silk, machine gun bullet cases and the top prize being a piece of a German bomber or fighter.

Parachute silk was prize booty and many a wedding dress and sets of undies were made from it.

I know for a fact that there was at least one unopened chute that had fallen out of an aircraft found in the Boreham Wood area and the exact spot is still not built on, I actually saw the wedding that the dress was made for.

The best time for obtaining the silk was during the Battle of Britain and the seven months of the *Blitz*, due to the number of aircraft shot down and number of parachute landmines that were dropped, the blast blowing large pieces of chute everywhere.

Later on in the book in the *'Service in the R.A.F.'* section I mention many of the redundant Lancasters at RAF Colerne, and when one of them was re-serviced the first place that was looked at for a forgotten chute was the rear-gunner's position as they were strapped to the framework just behind him and easily missed when de-boarding. The proceeds bought many a pint of beer in the local pub, or so I was told!

The Chicken Run

There was one particular incident I remember, sometimes vividly. While we were sleeping in the Anderson air raid shelter in Marlborough Road, loads of incendiary bombs were dropped and were starting fires everywhere.

One had fallen in our next door's garden and set fire to the chicken shed and run. Nobody was in next door and between the gardens there was a five-foot high brick wall with trellis on top. My Dad and Uncle Bill Johnson were trying to put the fire out with a stirrup pump through the trellis-work but could not reach the chicken run where the chickens were going mad, so being small I volunteered to climb over the wall and trellis to at least let the chickens out.

Mum was shouting for me not to go but by now I was astride the trellis-work when it collapsed. I screamed with pain, which made matters worse. I was wearing short trousers and the trellis had pinched the inside of the top of my thigh, I had the mark on my leg for a few years.

I managed to release the chickens and they scattered far and wide, well most of them did, a few did not make it; the smell of burning feathers is not very pleasant.

When the people next door returned later on in the day they came round to thank me, but thankfully they did not smell the chicken being roasted in Aunt Lizzie's oven.

The Pilot

Another incident I remember was one Saturday afternoon towards the end of September 1940 not long after we had arrived in Becontree. I had gone with my Dad and one or two of my Uncles to see a football match at a ground behind the *Merry Fiddlers* pub on the roundabout. The air raid sirens went about 2 pm and a dogfight was soon taking place high above us.

I was outside the pub, of course, and two or three aircraft were shot down. There were two parachutes floating down and by now all the occupants of the pub were outside looking up. Someone picked out the German airman, or so he thought. When he landed, which was right on the roundabout, he was set upon by a few of the crowd.

A bus driver, whose bus was parked on the stop, ran over to the green shouting that they had picked the wrong one. The pilot had broken his ankle on landing and by now had a bloody nose. The bus driver zipped open his flying suit to show his wings. He was in fact a *Polish* airman and the last I saw of him was when he was being carried shoulder high into the *Merry Fiddlers* pub.

Many years later, 1968 to be precise, we were on holiday in a guesthouse in Great Yarmouth. There were three families with children there and after dinner when we had put the children to bed we would sit in the small bar they had in the rear extension and just chat. For some reason or other I was telling this story when the landlady of the guesthouse was sitting with us having a drink. She suddenly stood up and said *"Oh my God, my parents lived in a house looking on to the Fiddlers roundabout"*. She went on to say that she was about five years old at the time and often thought that she had dreamt it all and this was the first time that the incident had been mentioned for over twenty-eight years. I assured her that it really did happen.

Another of my memories of this period is recalled whenever I smell snuff. Nanny O'Neill always had her *'twist'* of a half ounce of *Wilson's snuff* and in the confines of an Anderson air raid shelter, at times it was quite pungent.

Another hazard was when a raid was a bit heavier than usual. Aunt Liz Johnson would liberally sprinkle her holy water over all and sundry.

At times Nanny O'Neill and Aunt Lizzie's rosary beads would work overtime.

We were a very large family and at least ten homes were destroyed and many more damaged. The only casualties we had were Uncle Fred Marsh's two budgerigars who had their necks broken by blast and my Mum had her backside nipped by a piece of shrapnel when getting into the Anderson shelter, but we had lots of near misses between us so I suppose you could say that the holy water and rosary beads worked.

School

When the new school term began September 1940 brother Tom and I attended Erkenwald School in Becontree which was a real eye-opener for me.

The school was single storey, set in *grass* playing fields surrounded with small trees and plants. It also had its own football and cricket pitches and for the first time in my life I had school dinners!

I also saw the inside of a proper gymnasium for the first time and there was also a large assembly hall with a stage. There were indoor lavatories, not outside brick constructions with no roof.

In early April we were allocated a house off Bennetts Castle Lane, Ilford. It was the first house Mum and Dad had ever had but we never slept upstairs even once because of the bombing but under a large table Dad had made, using it as an indoor shelter which saved our lives.

This meant that we had to leave Erkenwald School as we were officially in the Borough of Ilford and were transferred to St Stephen's School which we both hated. Jerry soon solved this problem for us.

I had three sand bags full of *treasure* and buried them in our garden at No. 4 Farm Way, just off Bennetts Castle Lane. I have often wondered if they are still there, my grandson George would love them.

The Fateful Night

Easter Saturday, 19th April 1941 brought one of the heaviest air raids for some time, the first bombs came down at approximately 9 pm. We were all under the table, Mum, Dad, my brother Tom and our dog Mac, a little Highland Terrier. The front of the house just disappeared and for the next nine hours or so we watched the searchlights and gun flashes from under the table. Unbeknown to us just up the road on the corner of Longbridge Road there was a landmine hanging on its parachute caught in a tree in the garden of the local doctor (Doctor Stewart). One of the last bombs of the raid dropped near enough to detonate it, which then brought down the rest of the house.

My memories of that fateful time are mainly of our rescue that took place on Sunday morning and the disappearance of our dog Mac, who we never saw again. I have no memories of the Monday, but the Tuesday I do remember well as it was the day that we moved to what was to become my home town for the next sixty years.

Departure

During the time that we were living in Becontree, Nanny Marsh and her daughter, my Aunt May, had moved to a flat in Boreham Wood. On hearing of our plight she invited us to live with them until we could find alternative accommodation.

We had very little luggage. Although Mum and Dad had collected what they could from our house in Millwall most of the small stuff had been looted, not by the local residents, but by the rescue services who had been brought in from outlying areas. The larger items were put into storage, which was later destroyed by fire.

The bits and pieces they had managed to save were left behind in Becontree so I have nothing to remind me of my childhood, only memories.

Our journey to Boreham Wood was by bus. We caught a local bus to the Greenline coach terminal and I remember the journey through London. At the terminal we caught the coach that would take us to our new home in the Hertfordshire countryside.

I had enjoyed my short stay in Becontree in spite of *living* in an Anderson shelter a lot of the time. While there we were spending time with other members of the family and being *streetwise* I made many new friends.

Before concluding Part 1 of my story I decided to add a few nostalgic thoughts on revisiting Millwall shortly after the bombing and on subsequent occasions over the years.

I remember returning to Millwall with Mum a month or two after we had arrived in Becontree to see if there was anything we could possibly salvage. The terrace block was still standing and was left just as the bomb had hit it, the blast going through almost four houses up from ours on the corner.

We picked over the bits and pieces and went through cupboards but the looters had done a good job, there was nothing worth taking. It was a strange feeling walking through the rubble and trying to remember how it was. A few years later I was walking through the rubble in Hamburg and I must say with mixed feelings, which brought home the futility of war.

Each time I have returned to Millwall the *smallness* of the streets and houses that are left always amazes me. I can just about work out where our house was, now being in the middle of *Yuppyland*. My school, St Edmund's, is still there as was the church up to a few years ago.

Dad's old boozer *The Magnet and Dewdrop* has disappeared as have many others he used to frequent!

The first football pitch I played on is still there in the *New Park* as we called it. Also the first cricket strip I played on right next to the *Mudchute*.

 No doubt like many others I would love to wander around the *Island* as it was when I left there with the docks full of ships from all over the world, the various smells from the spice sheds and factories, the sounds of the tugs on the river, the dozens of horse drawn carts with stabling all over Millwall (Dad had some lovely roses), the various tradesmen selling their wares from handcarts or large wicker baskets, the *"Stop me and buy one"* Wall's Ice Cream seller, the pease pudding and faggots from the German butcher. The pie and mash shops with plenty of liquor not forgetting the jellied and stewed eels and as a special treat a glass of lemonade and an arrowroot biscuit sitting on the pub doorstep.

In those days it seemed as though we had much more time to enjoy the simple pleasures of life, going for walks, reading, indoor games, visiting family and friends, stopping in the street to enjoy a chat. Every lamp post had a wicket chalked on it and any blank wall had goal posts.

We had nothing and shared everything. Now we have everything and still want more. Television, among other things, has a lot to answer for.

"Scattered around the world are a small band of Londoners, unwilling or unable to rid themselves of the 1940/41 Blitz, despite the sixty or so years in which they have grown old, bent and weary; the Blitz is still there, in the dusty cellars of their minds. Sometimes it emerges, it might be a car back-firing, smoke rising from a burning building, fireworks going off, a clap of thunder, the sound of an air raid siren on television. Then the memories return."

Taken from "The Longest Night"
(Voices from the London Blitz)
By Gavin Mortimer (2005)

PART 2

1941 - Early 1950s

THE BOREHAM WOOD ERA

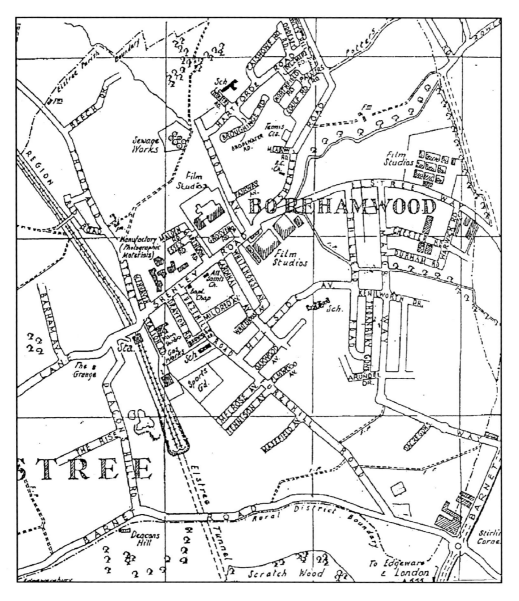

Map of Boreham Wood

c 1950

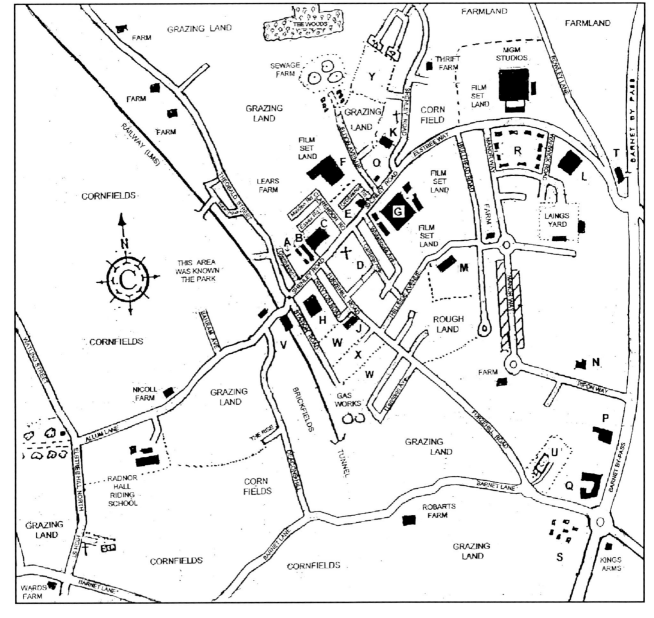

MAP OF BOREHAM WOOD 1939-1945

A	E.J. Freestone stables	N	Land Army Hostel
B	Dufay Works	O	Red Lion Public House
C	Keystone Works	P	RNLI
D	Council Offices	Q	Oppermans
E	Dutch Oven	R	Factories
F	Rock Studios	S	Caravan Corner
G	BIP Film Studios	T	Thatched Barn
H	Gate Film Studios	U	Home of Rest for Horses
J	Furzehill School	V	Elstree Station (LMS)
K	Studio Cinema	W	Allotments
L	Smiths	X	AA Sports Ground
M	Hillside School	Y	Meadow Rd, Playing Fields

During the 1940s Rock Studios became British National Studios and
BIP became ABPC - Associated British Picture Corporation

2.1 EARLY MONTHS IN BOREHAM WOOD

Dressed in the clothes that we had been wearing since the day of the rescue two days earlier, and with very little luggage, we arrived in Boreham Wood on Tuesday, 22nd April 1941. We alighted from the Greenline coach at the bus stop outside the old Furzehill Junior School. Nanny Marsh's upstairs flat at No 7 Brownlow Road was just around the corner. Mum, Tom and I soon settled in. Dad stayed at Becontree as he was still working in Millwall. It was a bit of a squeeze but there was a war on.

Mr Foley the local piano tuner lived with his family downstairs at No 7. I believe his daughter Mary still lives there. The other neighbours I remember were the *Fitzjohn* and *Hoy* families who became friends with our family. The *Goodwin* family lived in one of the cottages on the other side of the road.

Brownlow Road and the adjacent Drayton and Furzehill Roads look very much the same today as they did nearly seventy years ago, except for the cars parked in the street and a few new houses that have been built over the years.

The last house on the left at the top of Furzehill Road was occupied by the *Scott* family and was called *Toorack*. I checked recently but there is no name there now.

Furzehill Road , close to the bus stop where we alighted from the Greenline bus
Brownlow Road is the turning to the left by the telegraph pole.

(photograph - Elstree & Boreham Wood Museuml)

Brother Tom was sent to Hillside School, but I never did go to school full time again. My Mother had to undertake war work and was employed by Specialloid Ltd, an engineering firm making aircraft parts in requisitioned buildings on the Rock Studios site, now a BBC Television Studio, in Clarendon Road. Aunt May was also out at work. Nanny Marsh worked in the kitchen of the Milk Bar that later became the Grosvenor Restaurant. Grandad Marsh, who died in 1942, was partly disabled and so I was left to my own devices.

I think that this period was one of the happiest times of my life. By June 1941 the main London *Blitz* was over, Hitler having decided to invade Russia. The regular wailing of sirens and the need to take shelter became a memory, although sporadic raids over Boreham Wood did take place. I have fond memories of going to the Studio Cinema with Aunt May. I called her Aunt although she was only eight to nine years older than me. I remember discovering Boreham Wood, which was still only a large village, and the surrounding countryside. – I was in my element.

I was now living in the *'country'* but in a house instead of a tin hut as we did when in the hop fields. I remember seeing my first Magpie and thought it was an escaped parrot! Three to five minutes in any direction from Shenley Road and you were *'in the country'.*

One of the first places I found was the brickfields on the other side of the railway line. I used to get there by going through the allotments and the AA playing fields behind the Challenge Rubber Works in Drayton Road and going over the tunnel entrance. At the top of the bank between the tunnel and brickfields were the bottoms of the long gardens of the houses in Deacons Hill. You couldn't see the houses in Deacons Hill but there were plenty of chicken houses of a design I had never seen before. If you lifted the lids on the little boxes that were on the side of the chicken houses most of them had large brown eggs in them. The rationing at the time gave you one egg per week. Well!

No questions were ever asked as to where a regular supply of new laid eggs were coming from at home after I had explained that I had found them, which to my mind at the time I had, so if anybody reads this who lived in Deacons Hill on the railway side wondered why their egg production dropped you know the answer. They were never wasted. I did consider having roast chicken for Sunday lunch one day but the hens made too much noise when I tried to grab one. Shame!

Elstree Reservoir, a favourite haunt of mine during my early days in Boreham Wood

(photograph - Elstree & Boreham Wood Museuml)

I used to walk miles and soon found that the 306 Green Country bus dropped me off at the Fisheries Pub right on the Elstree Reservoir. What a magic place that was then, especially to a Cockney lad! Ducks eggs were soon on the menu, it being the right time of the year. I also discovered Aldenham Lake and spent many happy hours fishing there with very basic equipment, the bridge and the cave-like boathouse made it all very magical.

Writing about the reservoir reminded me of one of the local characters who lived in the cottages by the pub, *Nibby Marlborough* and his sister *Rose*. Nibby was an insurance collector around Boreham Wood and Elstree and always had a bottle of ink in the top pocket of his waistcoat and a large quill pen which he used to make the payment entry in the books, hence his nickname of *Nibby*. Other local characters: *Jack O'Brien* whose camp was at the side of the reservoir, *Neddy Joe* who camped at the bottom end of Radlett Road. *Mr Cosh* who had a caravan in *Coshes Wood* just off Green Street and the *Major* who patrolled the pubs from the *Wellington* to the *Elstree Way*. The story about the Major was that he was the black sheep of a wealthy family who gave him a monthly allowance to stay away.

During my first few weeks I had a brush with the local paperboy in Furzehill Road. He jumped off his bike, ran at me and said, *"We don't want any more of you townies here"* and thumped me. I thumped him back and we finished up on the ground. We were separated by a man standing at his front garden gate, maybe waiting for his paper, who I later found to be *Mr Barnes*, the father of *Joan Barnes* who later became one of my girl friends.

Eddie Evans 1945

The lad I had the punch up with was *Eddie Evans* who later became a legend playing football for Boreham Wood and cricket for Elstree. We later became good friends and have been for nearly sixty five years. I have written in detail about Eddie in the book I wrote on the history of Boreham Wood Football Club.

The other local lads I remember myself and brother Tom making friends with were *Ray Dawes* No 7 Clarendon Road, *Tommy Thompson*, No 5 Clarendon Road, *Ray Vaughan* No 10 Clarendon Road, *Don Carless* about No 19 Clarendon Road, *Bill Crossland* flats over Sainsburys, and then later *all of the lads* at E.J. Freestones and the Army Cadets.

As time went by I discovered the fields on the right going into Radlett along Theobald Street were where the best mushrooms grew; and no doubt they still do.

The easy ways into the various orchards were mostly along the railway line past Red Road and Theobald Street including the Convent, the Station Master's garden just over the railway bridge where I got caught once, and the back gardens of the six or so houses at the top of Cowley Hill on the left. So I even scrumped apples and pears from the house I eventually bought many years later!

After living in Brownlow Road for a few months, Aunt Rose, my Mum's youngest sister, came back to live because Mick, her husband, had been called up. By now we knew a few of the locals and Mum found a ground floor flat in No 8 Clarendon Road, which was between the three storey flats and Keystones wall. Dad then came back to live with us having gone back to his old firm, York Shipleys in Hendon. Mum now on night work was still working at Specialloids, which was right on her doorstep.

Within a very short time we were on the move again.

An end of terrace house No 9 right opposite where we were now living became available for rent from a couple who were having a trial separation, he was in the Army and his wife went back to live with her parents in Elstree. So for the first time in our lives as a family we went upstairs to bed, that was when we were not in the Anderson shelter in the garden. The second stage of the *Blitz* had started but it was nothing to compare with London and Dagenham.

We had short spells in the Anderson shelter when the *'Doodlebugs'* followed by the *'V2'* rockets came over but that did not last too long.

After about three months living in No 9 the couple decided to part, they gave Dad the rent book, moved their bits and pieces out and left us to it.

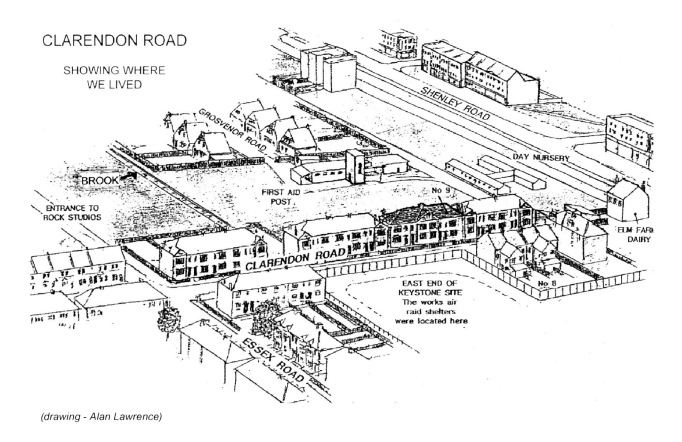

CLARENDON ROAD

SHOWING WHERE
WE LIVED

GROSVENOR ROAD

SHENLEY ROAD

DAY NURSERY

BROOK

ENTRANCE TO
ROCK STUDIOS

FIRST AID
POST

No 9

ELM FARM
DAIRY

CLARENDON ROAD

EAST END OF
KEYSTONE SITE
The works air
raid shelters
were located here

No 8

ESSEX ROAD

(drawing - Alan Lawrence)

Dad went down to Drayton Road to *Thomas Hughes*, the Estate Agents who were handling the property, to sort things out. I remember the rent was thirty shillings a week (£1.50).

Tommy Hughes told Dad that the tenancy could not be transferred as easy as that because he had somebody else in mind for the house.

Dad told Mr Hughes to call round next morning to sort it out, he called round about 10.30 next morning and Dad, having taken time off from work, did not answer the door but spoke to him from an upstairs window telling him that with what we had been through over the past year we were going nowhere. He told him that the neighbours would see to our needs if he decided to lay siege to the house with bailiffs. They did for a few days but eventually Tommy Hughes told Dad that he could stay. When my brother and I had to buy the house during the sixties to enable Mum and Dad to stay there Mr Hughes acted for us and when I bought my first house in Cowley Hill, he did the business for me.

I remember him telling me that he took the decision to let us stay in the house in Clarendon Road in 1941 after making a few enquiries as to our previous circumstances. So estate agents aren't all bad.

Mum and Dad saw their lives out in No 9 Clarendon Road. Dad passing on in 1978 and Mum on Christmas Day in 1983. Brother Tom died December 2003 aged 73 after losing his fight against lung cancer.

Mum and Dad outsde
No 9 Clarendon Road
1945

(photographs - Bill O'Neill)

Theobald Street in the 1940s.
Tommy Tompkins butcher's shop was close to where the car is parked.
His abattoir was on the opposite side of the road

(photograph - Elstree & Boreham Wood Museuml)

After spending my first few months in Boreham Wood exploring and exploiting I decided to find myself a job. *Tommy Tompkins* the butcher in Theobald Street, took me on as a delivery boy. I was provided with a heavy-duty tradesman's bicycle which had a large basket on the front in which I carried portions of rationed meat to Tommy's customers. In between deliveries I had to sit in the slaughterhouse on the opposite side of the road and pluck pheasants, a job that I hated. I remember feeling very unwell when I saw a pig being slaughtered; mind you Mum and Dad were very pleased with the lump of pork I took home to show them!

After a short period I had had enough of plucking pheasants and riding a trades bike around Boreham Wood so I went to work for *Elm Farm Dairies* on the corner of Clarendon Road. *Len Cook* was the proprietor and lived over the front shop with the dairy at the back in Clarendon Road. *Jim White* did all of the bottling and my Aunt Rose was for a time the bottle washer. *Len Cook*, his wife and young daughter lived above the shop. Jim White, who lived in Bullhead Road was quite a character and in fact gave me my first pair of long trousers; grey flannels. He also gave me a bicycle which allowed me to discover more of the outlying areas. *Jim Read* also worked there for a time as did *Tommy Smith* (Smith family, Shenley Road) until he went into the Navy and Jim Read into the Merchant Navy.

I worked on the milk round with *Len Cook* and our transport was a chariot-type horse drawn milk float; talk about *Ben Hur!* This was later replaced by a purpose-built four-wheeled milk-float (Green and White). The horse was stabled at Bill Munt's stables and riding school at Radnor Hall off Allum Lane where I got friendly with *Peter Munt*, Bill's son.

I had some very happy times there learning to ride and show-jump. The mounted section of the Home Guard stabled their horses there. A whole book could be written about that and would make a very good film, *"Horses and Sabres versus Tanks"* (week-ends only)! More of that later.

I bought my first pair of Jodhpurs and *Peter* gave me a pair of his old riding boots and I rode whenever I could. I also collected quite a few bruises when I started jumping.

The main gymkhana events were held in Cassiobury Park, Watford and I rode in a novice competition representing Radnor Hall Riding Stables and sponsored by Elm Farm Dairy.

I rode a horse called *Watford Lad*, a fourteen year old eighteen hands high, who had run in the Grand National some time in the mid thirties but I cannot remember his name at that time although *Windsor Lad* rings a bell; his new owner had renamed him *Watford Lad*.

The course for the event was four jumps up, and four jumps down twice round. I completed the first round with eight clear jumps, cleared the next four and at the turn I lost control. The horse getting the bit between his teeth, just turned down the middle of the course to the exit. The crowd across the exit parted to let the horse run through just as a woman pushed a large twin pram across the opening, saw what was happening and froze. So there was I, a fifteen year old, eight stone soaking wet lad on this very large horse, legs stuck straight out in front of me in the stirrups leaning back on the reins and having no effect whatsoever!

The horse cleared the pram by several feet, as I was told later, to great applause but I had no control of the horse at all until he stopped at our horsebox.

The ironical part of the story is that I had cleared twelve fences and the nearest to me had cleared eleven, but as I had not completed the course I was disqualified!

Apart from general stabling and the riding school, Munts supplied horses and various horse-drawn transport for the film industry. Just before the War they had worked on the film "*Love on the Dole*". While I was there the *Max Miller* and *Jenny Lind* film "*Good Evans*" was being shot at the *Rock Studios* in Clarendon Road.

The film was about horse racing and Max Miller was a bookmaker. In one of the scenes shot in a stable yard, Max was singing to Jenny Lind, standing at a stable door with a horse with its head over the door between them. The horse kept moving away from the door so we fitted a bar under its bridle and I sat behind the door holding the bar so that the horse stayed at the door. I did not even get a mention in the film's credits!

For some reason or other there was an elephant in the film controlled by a strongman named Samson, the elephant was stabled at Radnor Hall and was in the first stable next to the tack room. The problem was that the horses would not leave their stables to drink from the tank in the yard so we had to water them all by bucket, when the elephant did eventually go we had to scrub the stall out three times before a horse would go into it.

At the time Radnor Hall was billeting the officers of the London Irish Regiment, one of the officers got friendly with Bill Munt and used to walk over to the stables on a Sunday evening to walk through the path to the Artichoke Pub in Elstree Village. One evening he brought a dead duck with him and held it up to the elephant in his stall. The elephant turned its back on him and pressed his head and his trunk in the far corner of the stable, clearly distressed, everybody laughed.

The following Sunday evening the officer was standing by the stall where the elephant was stabled. It suddenly whipped the end of its trunk across his face splitting his cheek which needed ten stitches, nobody laughed!

Shenley Road looking east. The trade bicycles leaning against the fence belong to 'Hunt' the butcher.
The awning shading his shop window can be seen on right.
The bicycles were similar to those owned by Tommy Tompkins

(photograph - Elstree & Boreham Wood Museuml)

Left: Rock Studios

Photo taken from
our back garden in
Clarendon Road

Right: Clarendon Park

All Saints Sunday School
Maypole Dancing

Photo taken from the
upstairs window of our
house in Clarendon Road

Left: Meadow Park

Football in the 1940s

(photographs - Bill O'Neill)

There were three local dairies serving Boreham Wood during the War. Elm Farm Dairy was on the corner of Clarendon Road, their bottles having red lettering.

Lears Home Farm Dairy, their shop being in Shenley Road at the bottom of Glenhaven Avenue, the dairy being at Lears Farm in Theobald Street. Their bottles having green lettering.

Robarts whose farm and dairy were in Barnet Lane, their bottles had dark blue writing.

Daltons Farm was at the top of Allum Lane and served mainly Elstree.

Elm Farm Dairy collected their milk from two local farms, Kinch's Farm in Watling Street and Stockholms Farm in Butterfly Lane, Letchmore. It was collected by van by *Bob Paine* whose wife and family owned *The Old Firm Café*, helped by their daughter *Dorothy*. Their elder daughter *Ida* served in the W.A.A.F.S. Their young son *Brian* was tragically killed falling from his bicycle. The family lived in Bullhead Road having been evacuated from St Margaret's Bay on the South Coast due to the shelling of nearby Dover by the Germans from France.

Lears Home Farm Dairy had their own farm in Theobald Street; the old barn is still there. They also had milk from Brooklands Farm further down towards Radlett.

Robarts had their own large dairy farm in Barnet Lane. There was also Littlechilds Dairy Farm at Well End.

I believe that all three dairies topped up supplies from the Express Dairy depot in Whetstone. Milk more or less remained the same price throughout the War at four and a halfpence per pint (2p).

In and around Boreham Wood there were no fewer than twelve working farms plus Edwards Chicken Farm and Kennels at the Beeches in Theobald Street. The 'V' of land formed by Shenley Road and the Elstree Way that now houses the Civic Offices, the swimming pool, Oaklands Hotel and the Studio housing estate right up to the MGM Studios was all cornfields. When the corn was cut in August, rabbits were shot from the Elstree Way.

Our near neighbours in Clarendon Road were:	
No 1	Mr & Mrs Allison and their son Alfie. They owned the Elstree Radio Shop in the village.
No 3	Mr & Mrs Dyer and their son Charlie, who had been living in Boreham Wood for some years. Mr Dyer had a brother who lived on Millwall and one of his sons, Albert, married my Mother's sister Flo. They moved to No 36 Melrose Avenue in Boreham Wood in 1938 and that is how the Boreham Wood connection was made.
No 5	The Thompsons had two sons.
No 7	The Dawes family. Mrs Dawes was a post lady who had three sons and a daughter. Alan was a Marine, Jim was in the Navy, and Ray who was about my age and Evelyn. Both Jim and Alan married A.T.S. girls who were billeted in Hollywood Court. Jim later played football for Boreham Wood as did two of his sons. They also had a lodger, Matt, who used to play the piano at weekends in the Mops and Brooms pub.
No 9	Our family, the O'Neills.
No 11	Mr & Mrs Treacher and their daughter Ann
No 13	The Thackers and their daughter Barbara.

	Further down the road, by the Brook and before the entrance to Rock Studios, were the Carless and Urqhuart families. On the opposite side of the road in the flats were the Fishers and their daughter Jean. In the houses between the flats and Keystones wall lived the Vaughans and their son Ray. Next door was the brother and his wife of Mr Dyer who lived in No 3 and the father of my Uncle Albert mentioned earlier. They had been bombed out from Millwall at the same time as us.
No 12	On the other side of the Keystones wall and beside the Brook were the Woosters, evacuees from South London who became family friends.
	A bit further down on the corner of Essex Road another of my Mother's sisters, Rose, married to Mike Webb also bombed out from Cubitt Town.
	In Essex Road names I remember were the Gannons in No 1 and their daughter Nellie. In No 3 Vic Bryant and his family, opposite were the Davis family, the Heron family, the Bradmans. Mrs Bradman was always known as Caravan Kate having lived in a caravan in the Studios for many years.
	In No 6 lived Nanny Marsh having moved from Brownlow Road.
	Other names around the bottom of Clarendon Road, Essex Road and Maldon Road were Belshaw, Leslie, Earwood, Woods whose sons, Colin and Peter, later played for the Wood, and the Websters.

The fields behind Maldon Road were known as the *'back fields'*. A large area of the fields were used as film set land and various film sets were built on them. One set was for the film *"Old Mother Riley goes to the Circus"*. A stick of bombs fell on the fields and we had great fun playing in the craters. There was a gate and stile entrance to the fields from Theobald Street opposite the convent.

Early in 1942 I was *'head hunted'* by *Janie Freestone* of the Dutch Oven to go and work for him on the bread rounds and so another very enjoyable chapter of my life began.

The other roundsmen that were there when I joined were *Jim Warner, Sean Brady, Peter Horrod* and *Joe Brady*. Within a short time of my going there *Jim Warner* went into the Army, *Sean Brady* into the Navy and *Peter Horrod* was called up as a *Bevan boy* and went to work in the coal mines in Wales where he met his wife to be and finished up living there. They were replaced by *John Tester, Sidney Hoy* and later *John Seviour*.

We had four separate bread rounds. The baker's carts were kept at the Dutch Oven. The yard area where the carts were kept was latterly an Italian Restaurant, formerly Signor Baffis. The horses were stabled at the top of Glenhaven Avenue opposite Clarendon Hall along with some riding horses. Putting the carts away entailed pushing them into the front yard by the shafts backwards, swing round sharp left to get them in place. The first time I did it I went in shafts first, could not swing round in time and the shafts went through the windows of the bake house, just missing *Len Perkins*, the confectioner, and spraying his prep table with glass. While Len was swearing at me, *Joe Brady* and company were doubled up with laughter.

The working horses were *Big John, Dobbin, Tom, Molly, Kitty* and *Pinto*. The riding horses were *Monty, Goldie, Dainty* and later *Misty*.

WORKING WITH EJ's HORSES

(photograph - Liz Stoneman)

(photograph - Bill O'Neill)

Above

Joe Brady driving the trap to the wedding of 'EJ's daughter Pat. Her sister Kath, with daughter Valerie and Miss Ferris (EJ's book-keeper) are seated in the back.

Above Right

Bill O'Neill with the trap in the road outside the stables in Glenhaven Avenue.

Right

John Tester on 'Goldie' with 'Monty'
Meadow Road   1944

(photograph - Bill O'Neill)

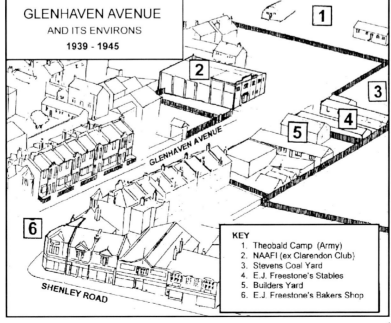

GLENHAVEN AVENUE
AND ITS ENVIRONS
1939 - 1945

KEY
1. Theobald Camp (Army)
2. NAAFI (ex Clarendon Club)
3. Stevens Coal Yard
4. E.J. Freestone's Stables
5. Builders Yard
6. E.J. Freestone's Bakers Shop

(drawing - Alan Lawrence)

We used to ride to and from the stables on the horses so I had to learn to ride bareback, which feels entirely different without a saddle. Imagine doing that today down Shenley Road.

Apart from the bake house there was the restaurant and shop, *Miss Bigsby* ran the restaurant, *Dorothy Kellock*, the waitress. Serving in the front shop were *Eva Kellock*, Dorothy's sister, and *Betty Page*. Next door to the shop and part of the main building was Jean's Dress Shop run by *Eve Oliver*, who I took out a few times but we never quite made it.

Janie Freestone lived above the restaurant and shop with *Mrs Freestone*, his two daughters *Kath* and *Pat* and son *John* who became friends with all of the roundsmen. Pat and Kath both married Coldstream Guards *Bernard* and *Laurie* who were stationed at Radnor Hall during the early part of the War. John married *Jean*, a Land Army girl working on Edwards Farm.

In the bakehouse apart from the governor were *Len Perkins* the confectioner, *George Clinton* a master baker, *Bobby Fitzjohn* and three Spanish lads, evacuees from the Spanish Civil War who lived in a hostel opposite the Gate Pub in Arkley. Their names were *Roberto, Jose* and *Manuel* otherwise known as *Bob, Joe* and *Jim*

The night bakers were *Reg Barker* from Elstree and *Cecil Hills* from Green Street. The bookkeeper, whose office was on the roof of the bakehouse, was *Miss Ferris* who lived in Grosvenor Road. We were one big happy family and all good friends.

My first official week's wages for a five and a half day week, but all day Saturdays, was seven shillings and sixpence (37 and a half pence). This was given as three half crowns in a small brown envelope with my name on it. I gave it to my Mum who over the years often mentioned the fact that she still had that envelope with the three half crowns in it. After Mum had died December 1983 my wife and sister-in-law Jean were sorting out in the house in Clarendon Road and they came across the envelope with the three half crowns in it.

When they gave it to me I thought *"Oh good, there will be three pre-war half crowns in it."* On inspection they were dated 1959, 1963 and 1967. What she had been doing was "borrowing and replacing" as required. It reminded me of pawnshop days.

Our day started at 8 am mucking out the horses, feeding and watering, harnessing them up and riding them down to the Dutch Oven, pulling the carts out and putting the horses in the shafts. Loading the carts with bread, flour, cakes and any special orders and going out to our rounds before 10 am.

The average round took about three hours. My two rounds were Mondays, Wednesdays and Fridays, Bullhead Road, Manor Way, Kenilworth Drive, Dacre Gardens and Hillside Avenue.

In those days the houses in Manor Way ended at the junction with Kenilworth Gardens. Between the junction right up to Dacre Gardens, six houses only, was the Laing Timber Workshops making army huts. Bullhead Road continued up from Kenilworth Drive for a bit longer. I also served Laings Canteen, which was then half-way up Bullhead Road on the right from the Elstree Way and Standard Telephone Canteen in Chester Road.

The Tuesday, Wednesday and Saturday round was Drayton Road, Brownlow Road part of Furzehill Road, Cardinal and Whitehouse Avenues.

In between we would, between us, take the bread and long cakes to Aldenham Schools in Letchmore Heath including Mrs Timms Tuck Shop which was in the school grounds, and to the BBC Overseas Foreign Broadcasting Service that is now part of Haberdashers Askes School. We used to go through the white gates at the bottom of Allum Lane passing the gatehouse where a family lived whose name I can't remember, but the daughter married one of the Baker family from Shenley Road. Then across the bridge over the lake, through the very well kept gardens to the large *secret* house, out the back way into Aldenham Road and down to the schools and back the same way. We were never challenged.

Around about March 1944 a *'horsey'* lady named *Veronica* joined us with a view to starting a riding school from the Glenhaven stables; in between times she helped out on the rounds when we were short.

Plans were prepared, submitted and passed by the Elstree Rural District Council to make alterations to the existing stables.

A copy of the plan of the intended alterations to the stables, together with other plans submitted by 'EJ' to the Council before WWII were sent to me recently by Alan Lawrence of Elstree and Boreham Wood Museum. They were very interesting, and apart from bringing back many memories, prompted me to make the two sketches that are included in this chapter and also add a couple of paragraphs about memories of the Grosvenor Restaurant in later years.

The alterations did not go ahead but *Veronica* decided to have a change round, she put all of the working horses into a general stable with kickboards between the horses and put all of the riding horses into the loose boxes. Our working horses did not like this and neither did we so every time she changed them over, we changed them back again. In the end we won. I don't remember anybody ever hiring riding horses from the stables.

Some Sunday mornings during the summer months, if we were not on Cadet duty, we would harness up the four wheeled trap and pick up the guv'nor, Janie Freestone. Usually there would be John Tester, Sid Hoy, Joe Brady and myself. Mr Freestone would always bring his twelve-bore shotgun; we would drive around the London Colney area, Silver Hill, Ridge and Mymms calling at one or two pubs along the way usually finishing up at the Black Horse pub in Shenley until closing time. We would have ginger wine and arrowroot biscuits brought out to us at regular intervals.

The usual procedure after leaving the pub was to drop off the guv'nor when passing the Dutch Oven. On one particular occasion we were coming down Cowley Hill on our way back to the stables when he saw a couple of crows in the branches of the large oak tree that stood at the junction of Potters Lane and Shenley Road. We were travelling at a fast trot when the guv'nor took aim. We shouted to him not to but he let go with both barrels. A shower of branches came down; the horse, Big John, took off at a gallop!. Joe Brady had the reins but could not hold him. He galloped along Shenley Road and took the turning after the Studio Cinema on two wheels. We flashed past the Dutch Oven with Mrs Freestone and her two daughters standing on the balcony awaiting our return. We carried on through the village and managed to get the horse under control just after crossing the railway bridge. I don't remember us passing one vehicle in Shenley Road; we changed horses and took the *guv'nor* home. As we dropped him off he asked, *"Did I get the crows?"*

Some Saturday evenings during the summer three or four of us along with the guv'nor and usually his son John, Joe Brady and myself would go over to Speyers Lake for pigeon shooting. He would have the 12 bore double-barrelled shotgun and we would have the 410's single barrel. We would hide just inside the fir trees around the lake and wait for the pigeons to come into roost. We always came back with pigeons and very often we would bake a pigeon pie in the bakehouse, making our own pastry. John would borrow a couple of bottles of beer from his Dad and we would warm up any left-overs in Miss Bigsby's fridge and sit in the bakehouse with a feast fit for a king.

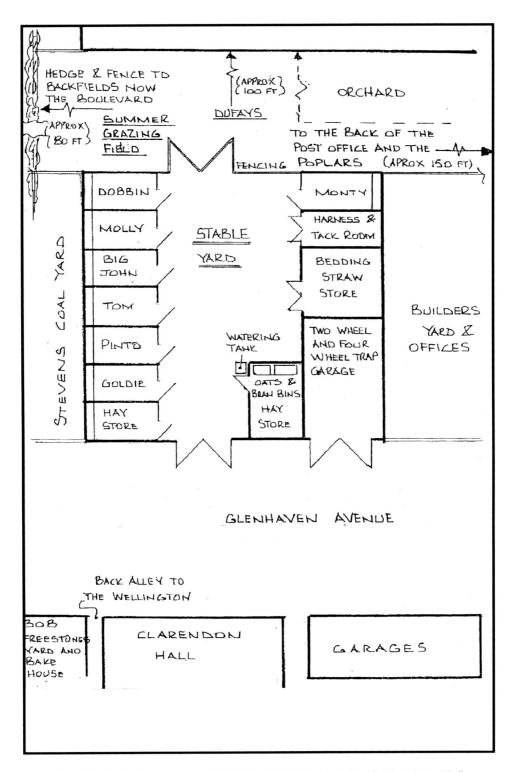

PLAN OF E.J. FREESTONE'S STABLES

GLENHAVEN AVENUE

c1939-1945

**My drawing is based on an original plan of the stables.
It is not to scale but shows how the buildings were used around the stable yard.
Each horse had a name and had its own stable.**

(drawing - Bill O'Neill)

On one of my visits to Elstree and Boreham Wood Museum to discuss the printing of this book with Alan Lawrence we paid a visit to the old stable buildings at the top of Glenhaven Avenue which are now used as workshops and garages. We were walking around and taking photographs when one of the chaps there enquired as to what we were doing. We explained about my involvement in the stables, he then told us that his father was an old Boreham Woodonian and was working in one of the old stables. We went in and found him and after a few minutes of conversation we discovered he was the nephew of Ted Thacker who had lived at No 11 Clarendon Road before, during and after the War and I, of course, knew Mr Thacker and his family quite well.

The stable we were standing in still had the concrete manger there and I remembered it was the same stable where the following incident occurred around 1943/44.

One of the horses was being clipped trace high, that is along the middle of his body, which always happened at the start of the summer. This particular horse did not like it and was kept under control by the use of a 'twitch', which was a round length of wood about one inch thick and one foot long with a hole through the top in which a loop of cord was fixed. It was then put over the horse's bottom lip and twisted until the horse realised that if he kept still it would not be twisted tighter. Sidney Hoy was sitting on the manger holding the twitch and I was sitting beside him. The horse started to play up, Sid increased the twitch, the cord snapped and the horse reared up and brought his front legs down on Sid's head and pawed at him several times until we managed to bring it under control. By now Sid was unconscious on the floor of the stable covered in blood. John Tester got the horse out of the stable and I ran over to the Clarendon Hall and the Army Sergeant on duty there summoned a first aid crew from the Theobald Street camp who bandaged *Sid* up and got him to Barnet Hospital. He took the four long scars on his head to his grave but it never put him off horses. He was taken on by the Jockey, Harry Wragg at his stables at Newmarket where Sid rode for him until he went into the Army. One of the winners he rode was *Anchors Aweigh* at Alexandra Palace, the old *Dripping Pan* track.

My sketch of the *Dutch Oven* was inspired by a plan submitted by EJ in 1939. It showed proposed alterations, mainly to the bakery, where new ovens were installed and an office built on the flat roof. All these alterations were completed and were as I remember them during the early forties. Another plan dated 1936 showed internal alterations to E J Freestone's shop on the corner of Glenhaven Avenue. It showed a shop on the ground floor with a large meeting room upstairs, which later became a restaurant. We had our wedding reception there in August 1952. The catering was carried out by *Josef* from the Grosvenor Hotel and Restaurant.

The bill for the wedding reception, signed by Josef, makes interesting reading re the prices:

1 two-tier wedding cake £5.10s.0d.

When the Grosvenor Restaurant and the Freestones shops were taken over by South Eastern Bakeries Ltd, the restaurant was being run by *Hill and Simmons Ltd* and Josef was Manager at the Grosvenor, until he became the owner of the restaurant and hotel. If my memory serves me right he did this at the request of ABPC Studios as there were no restaurant facilities in the Studios until much later.

I became a regular customer at the Grosvenor over the years and made good friends with Josef and Myra. The headwaiter at the time was *Terry* and when he left, *Constantine* one of the Spanish waiters, took over.

Josef was an Austrian prisoner of war who stayed on in England when the War ended. They had one daughter, *Margaret,* and they lived in Red Road off Theobald Street. He always rode a bike to and from work.

One incident I remember involving Josef was around 1969/70 when a party of us dined at the restaurant to celebrate one of our anniversaries. After leaving the restaurant we all went up to brother *Tom's* house in Featherstone Gardens to finish off. Just as we arrived there my wife realised that she had left the presents we had been given behind so I said I would drive back to the Grosvenor and pick them up. It was about 11.30 pm on a Sunday evening, I drove down Manor Way and turned into the Elstree Way just in front of a police car. I had been drinking. I thought they would turn into the police station that we had to pass, but no; slight panic. I turned left into Whitehouse Avenue, so did they; more panic. I turned left behind the shops to park in the small car park behind the restaurant, so did they; real panic!. I pulled up outside the back entrance to the restaurant, so did they; total panic!. I got out of my car, so did they. I walked towards the restaurant; they totally ignored me and went into the back of the Chinese restaurant that was next door to the Grosvenor. As I walked in *Josef* met me and asked, *"Bill, what is the matter? You look a bit pale."* I told him the story and his first words were, *"Sit down while I get you a Brandy!"* I told him what he could do with his Brandy.

We still have two of the Mother-in-Law's Tongue plants he gave us that he used to grow for display in the restaurant bar.

Returning to the bakery, sometimes the rounds changed around a bit and at times I served Allum Lane, about twelve houses in Barham Avenue quite a few of the houses on the left being used as Army Officer's billets, Deacons Hill, and about ten houses in The Rise.

The price of a large loaf of bread throughout the War was the same as for a pint of milk; again four and a half pence (2p). I don't ever remember having a lunch then known then as a dinner break; we had rolls, buns and cakes on board and when Miss Bigsby wasn't looking we would nick some butter or margarine from her fridge.

When the rounds were finished we would go back to the Dutch Oven, unload the van, pay in, take the horse out of the cart, put the cart away, ride the horse back to the stables, unharness, wipe him down, feed and water, and depending on the time put his bed down, about 5.30/6.00 pm, lock up and go home. In between we had to keep the carts clean, oil and polish the harness, and keep a general eye on the horses healthwise. When they needed shoeing we would ride them up to Albert Sands, the blacksmith, in Elstree High Street.

The winter shoes had two tapped holes in the heel of the shoe so that in icy and snowy weather we could screw *'roughs'* into them; these were wedge shape pieces of iron that enabled the iron shoe to get a grip in ice.

The horses knew their rounds very well and if you stayed too long at one house they would move on.

We were instructed, when the air raid sirens went, to remove the horse from the shafts and hitch him to the back wheels and then find shelter but when we were getting three or more warnings per day we did not bother, we just stayed with the horse. If there was an extra heavy air raid at night with plenty of anti-aircraft fire very often John Tester and myself would go up to the stables and calm them, a few stale rolls usually did the job.

One of the worst jobs working with horses was when one had to be put down, remember this was wartime Britain and all services were stretched to their limit. The vet would be called in and as there was not the treatment there is today it was kinder to call in the knackers' man to do the job at the stables on the vet's advice. During my time there we had four horses put down – Kitty, Big John, Dobbin and Tom. Either John Tester or I held their head in the yard, we would close the top doors on the stables where the other horses were and with the humane bolt gun the job would be done. They would then be winched into the back of the lorry. John Tester and I shed many a tear. They were our friends and workmates.

It was fun working at the Dutch Oven. I don't ever remember getting a rise over the years but when 'booking in' there always seemed to be a surplus that would cover a cup of tea and a bun or two at the Old Firm Café and a ticket for the cinema!

I carried on working for E J Freestone until my call-up to the R.A.F. in 1945.

PLAN OF THE DUTCH OVEN
AND THE SURROUNDING AREA c.1940

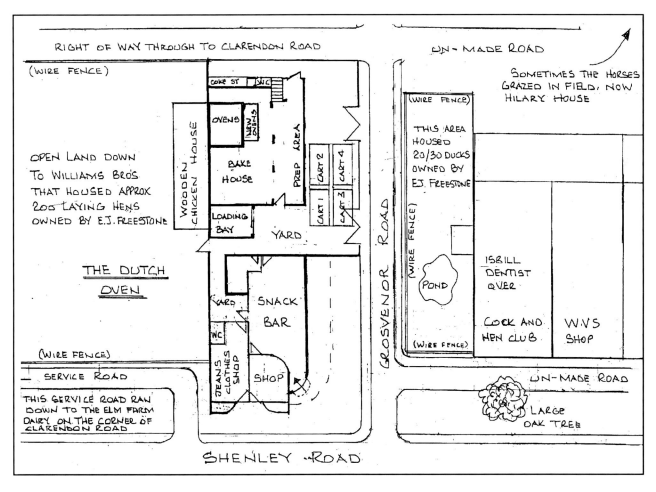

(drawing - Bill O'Neill)

I referred to the information that E.J. Freestone submitted to the council for planning approval when I drew the above plan. My drawing shows the layout of the, premises and the area where we kept our delivery carts. It also shows how 'EJ' made good use of the adjacent waste ground, on which he kept hens and ducks during the Second World War.

Above the bakehouse was the flour store and the route to the office on the flat roof over the loading bay. The flour was emptied from the sacks, down a shute into the mixing drums. Being right over the ovens it was always very warm up there and coming off the rounds after a wet day we could warm and dry off before getting soaked again riding the horses back to their stables in Glenhaven Avenue.

MEMORIES OF OUR WEDDING DAY

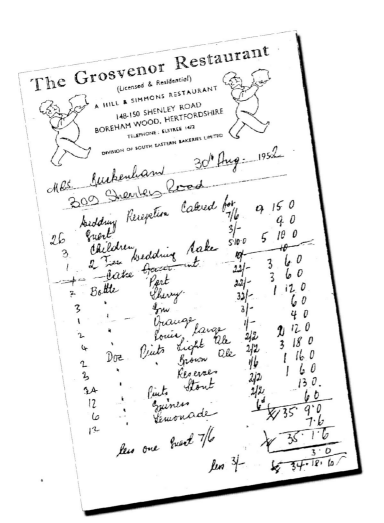

Bill for our
Wedding Reception
Catering

... and the Receipt

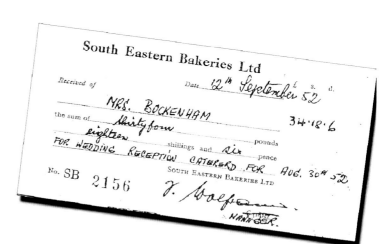

2.3 ARMY CADETS AND HOME GUARD

About the middle of 1942 a branch of the Army Cadet Corps was started (*E. Battery, Royal Artillery*) meeting at the old Furzehill Road School. Twice mid week, evenings and Sunday mornings.

The Officers were *Captain Johnson, Major Mumford* and *Under Officer Skuse.* The Sergeant was a member of the local Home Guard who lived in Edgware.

Some Cadets whose names I remember:

Peter Parkins	Joe Brady	George Ray
Barry Bowen	Jackie Bolton	Ray Dawes
Reg Hickey	John McEvoy	Tony Asherwood
Eddie Evans	Carl Wilkinson	Tiger Smith
Digger Spriggs	Bluey Wilkinson	Tony Sharp
Brian Sutton	Colin Curry	

Again from memory the unit was about forty strong.

We were taught arms drill, field craft, compass and map reading, marching drill and weaponry. We did our rifle range training at the drill hall in Barnet.

We met twice every week, on parade at 7.00 pm and went on weekend manoeuvres, being dropped off in the country from army lorries. We had to get to certain map points the next day and attack areas defended by the local Home Guard. The two areas we were usually dropped in were Berkhampsted or Hoddesdon. After the attack and debriefing we arrived home mid afternoon on the Sunday tired out and starving. If there had been an air raid in progress then it gave more reality to the exercise.

After a couple of years we were quite well trained and could look after ourselves and good friendships developed.

I remember one exercise in particular when we had to defend the Tee-Woods, now Grove Road, Crown Road and part of Gateshead Road, against the local Home Guard one Sunday morning. We guessed they would be coming in the direction of Boreham Wood i.e. down Eldon Avenue, past the sewage works to attack the upside down part of the Tee

On the Saturday night a few of us went up to the woods, broke and bent a few branches over, hung a few bits of webbing about, trampled the grass up to and along the line of the trees to give the impression that we were there waiting for them.

The whole Cadet Unit then arrived an hour earlier to take up a camouflaged position behind the ammunition sheds that were at the bottom of Eldon Avenue between the end of the maisonettes and the sewage works.

The Home Guard arrived, received their orders to spread along the northern perimeter of the sewage works and at 10 am precisely the very pistol was fired to start the '*battle*'.

As they prepared to move forward we went through the observers and umpires with our blanks firing and thunder flashes being thrown at the advancing Home Guard from behind who just stood there looking at us. Whistles were blown by the umpires, the Home Guard Officers were protesting and we were claiming victory. By 10.15 am it was all over. A post mortem was held and the point was made that we, the Cadets, had an unfair advantage by knowing from which direction the attack on the woods would be made. We won the day by claiming that the Home Guard could have attacked from any direction but chose the obvious and our gamble came off. We were declared the *winners*. I have often thought that the whole incident would have made a lovely *"Dads Army"* episode.

Janie Freestone was in the Home Guard and he let them use the stables in Glenhaven Avenue for rifle practice using air-guns and two-twos. They used to lie down behind the sand bags at the entrance gates and shoot down the length of the yard at targets pinned on the fence, behind which was a great pile of horse manure which stopped the bullets going any further.

He also kept all of the sweepings from the floor of the bakehouse, mainly flour, put into small linen bags which were then used for hand grenade practice. Quite often the bags split and if the horses didn't lick the flour up, the rats soon did.

One incident that nearly backfired was when three or four Home Guard were on guard one night at the Elstree railway tunnel and someone had the idea of playing a joke on them by lowering a cardboard box with an old alarm clock in it down to the tunnel entrance. From what I was told of the incident only a few years ago it was pure *"Captain Mannering"* and the *"Don't Panic, Don't Panic"* could have come from that night.

The pranksters were a couple of well-known local lads on leave from the Army who were commandos having their usual night in the saloon bar of the Crown Public House. Any ideas who this might have been?

On another occasion the Home Guard and the Cadets put on a display in the backfields. An hour or so before the display was due to start a mixed number were camouflaged in the grass in full kit with their rifles pointing at the chairs and forms where the spectators would be sitting and on an order would suddenly stand up hopefully to great applause.

Unfortunately some of the families had brought their dogs with them and you can guess what happened next. They sniffed them out and danced round them barking, there must have been many similar incidents all over the country at the time; hence the popularity of "Dads Army".

No doubt if Jerry had invaded then all those involved with the Home Guard and Cadets would have done their bit where possible. As the threat of invasion diminished towards the end of 1944 the Home Guard, in particular, held less parades etc.

The Army Cadets also had a good football team and *Barry Bowen* and myself were the first two Cadets in Hertfordshire to get the award of War Certificate A. The test being taken over three weekends at Welwyn Garden City and I was made up to Sergeant. The first exercise I took part in as a Sergeant was to attack a Regular Army unit which was in a wooded area in Berkhamsted very early one Sunday morning. We were dropped off approx. 6.00 pm on the Saturday evening about ten miles away, given map references and left to it. We were loaded up with blank ammo plus plenty of thunder flashes. We were told that there would be plenty of booby traps around the camp in the shape of trip wires. We were also told which building was the mess hall and if we managed to *'contain'* the camp we would have breakfast before the troops as our victory prize.

There were twenty four in the unit; we decided to split up into four squads and approach from four different directions. We were in position at 4.00 am the attack being timed for 5.00 am. We moved forward very cautiously and well camouflaged. We did not come across one booby trap but there were plenty of signs that the area surrounding the camp had been trodden down.

At 5.00 am in almost full daylight we rushed the camp throwing thunder flashes and firing into doors and windows with no response. It was Sunday, 4 June 1944. The whole camp had moved out on the Friday to move south for the invasion and nobody had informed the Cadet HQ. So no breakfast and a five hour wait for our transport home.

One of the perks for the older Cadets was taking the white Cadet flashes out of our hats. We would go to the dances and NAAFI Club at the Clarendon Hall in Glenhaven Avenue. There was dancing to records most nights and sometimes I played the piano there. A local band usually played on a Saturday evening.

The mounted Home Guard were about a dozen strong and usually held their parade in the Rock Studios. When darkness fell and they were still out they had red reflector lights on elasticated tape which they put on the horses tails, it was quite funny to see a dozen or so red lights bobbing away along Shenley Road. What they were supposed to do if Jerry had invaded God only knows.

One Bank Holiday Monday they took part in a recruitment drive with the Home Guard and Cadets on the backfields and one of their displays was to gallop past stakes in the ground with a large turnip on top and slice through them with their swords as they passed.

Len Cook scored a direct hit for the first time but followed through, his sword going deep into the stake and so pulling him out of the saddle. He was limping for weeks and never tried it again.

On one or two occasions a rider would become unseated and one of three things would happen. The horse would just stand and graze, gallop off to be caught by one of the other riders, or as sometimes happened, just go back to Radnor Hall and stand outside its stable in the yard. The fallen rider would 'double up' or wait for someone to bring a car back, usually Bill Munt, to pick him up.

Most of the horses were kept at the Radnor Hall stables. Not all of the mounted Horse Guard owned their own horses. The owners lent them to the Home Guard usually one night per week and over most weekends, I earned many a shilling shining their coats and painting their hooves black before a parade. There were very few grass fields where they could go for a good gallop due to the need to grow food. After the harvest they had more choice for a short period, but I noticed they only picked the nice flat fields.

The mounted detachment wore flat caps with the strap under their chin when they drew sabres and charged. They used to start off in line abreast and over a one hundred yard gallop never did cross the finishing line in a line, being spread out over ten to fifteen yards. It always seemed as though the biggest blokes were on the smaller horses. The one horse I remember most was *Red Rose*, a chestnut mare who was owned by *Sandy Powell's* first wife who lived in the first bungalow past Hillside School and could often be seen riding through Boreham Wood.

I remember one occasion in particular when there was a joint exercise involving the Home Guard, the Cadets and the Mounted Home Guard. We were told not to let the thunder flashes off too near the horses as it frightened them! I hope somebody would have told Jerry if he had invaded!

Furzehill School where the army cadets met for training

Boreham Wood Home Guard Platoon pose for a group photograph at Rock Studios
Note the Mounted Section at rear.

(photographs - Elstree & Boreham Wood Museuml)

2.4 OTHER WARTIME MEMORIES OF BOREHAM WOOD

Living in Boreham Wood during the War years was good fun with plenty to do apart from staying alive. From the outbreak of the War, members of the Armed Forces were billeted in the vicinity and by the time I came to Boreham Wood in 1941 until hostilities ceased the locals regarded it as a garrison town. The service personnel boosted the population of the town and used many of the facilities in the area.

Dancing was a particularly popular leisure time pursuit that was shared with the local people.

Why H.M. Forces were in the area

At the time a large part of the local area was farmland, parts of which were regularly used by famous regiments for infantry and mechanised warfare training. Other service men and women operated in the area on a wide range of activities including:

- manning anti-aircraft batteries and other defensive devices

- working in military stores,

- operating wireless stations etc.

Listed below are some of the units that were here after I came.

- The Pioneer Corps in the two Army camps in Theobald Street.

- The London Irish Regiment at Radnor Hall.

- The R.A.F. at Radlett and Letchmore Heath.

- The Royal Corps of Signals at Shenley.

- The R.A.F. Link Trainers in Manor Way.

- A.T.S. girls were billeted in Hollywood Court, W.A.A.F.s in Barnet Lane.

- W.R.N.S. at Arkley and Land Army girls in Ripon Way.

General Services

There was no police station in Boreham Wood, just a police box and an air raid siren in Shenley Road close to Elm Farm Dairies. The main police station was in Barnet and there were smaller police Stations in Elstree and Shenley villages. The three local policemen that I remember were *Messrs. Johns, Smith* and *Bruce*.

The main fire station in the area was in the B.I.P. studios. Sub-stations were located in Elstree and Shenley.

In the latter part of the War a new fire station was built in Manor Way.

A.R.P., later Civil Defence, personnel were originally located in various empty buildings in the town and the First Aid Section took over the Church Hall. Later a new control centre was built on the site of the present cinema and a large first aid building was built in Clarendon Park. It later became the library. The Church Hall was converted into a *British Restaurant* where you could get a basic three course meal for one shilling; (5p).

There were three schools – Furzehill, Hillside and the private Sion Catholic school adjacent to the convent in Red Road.

The only doctors that I can remember were Dr. Daly at the top of Furzehill Road and Dr. Winter in Shenley Road, on the corner of Clarendon Road. His daughter Dagmar became a Hollywood film star, Dana Wynter, and starred in films such as *"D-Day Sixth of June"* with *Robert Taylor* and *Richard Todd, "Sink the Bismark" and many others.*

Industry

The local farms were having to make full use of their land for growing crops and there were many Land Army girls working in the fields.

Most of the factories were either fully or partly engaged in war work. The Challenge Rubber Works and Victaulic Engineering firms worked to full capacity. Many people were employed at Smiths, Kautex and The Henderson Safety Tank Company and were working two-shift seven-day weeks.

Parts of Keystone Knitting Mills were taken over by de Havillands for the manufacture of components for their *Mosquito* bomber. The adjacent Dufay Photographic Works was almost totally engaged on war work. Oppermans Engineering was full out on general engineering work. There were also many small companies doing their bit. It meant that during the war there was always full employment in Boreham Wood and that you could walk straight out of school at the age of fourteen and get a job, as most did.

Only one of the four local film studios was able to make films during the war. B.I.P. later A.B.P.C. and the GATE were taken over by the R.A.O.C. for the duration mainly for use as Army stores; although other military work, some of a secret nature, was also carried out there. Amalgamated Studios later M.G.M. was taken over by the Ministry of Health for the storage of their records and by Handley Page who built parts for the Halifax bomber there.

Rock Studios later British National in Clarendon Road did make some films during the War in spite of the fact that most of their buildings were taken over for war work.

During the war period, Bill Munt had a contract to convey items between the two studios that were being used by the R.A.O.C. He had four double horse and carts continually going between the two sites transferring boxes of stores which were loaded and unloaded by soldiers of the Pioneer Corps. I am convinced that when they moved the boxes from one studio, they took them all back again! Many others shared my opinion.

Public Transport

Apart from the all-steam LMS Railway to London and St Albans and beyond we had the red buses. The No 141 went from Elstree Way to Edgware Tube Station via Elstree Village, which cost two and a half pence, and the 107 from Ponders End to Drayton Road via Barnet.

There was the Green double-decker country bus No 306 from East Barnet Station to Watford Junction via Boreham Wood, Elstree and Bushey; there were about two per day, the 311 from Drayton Road to Watford via Shenley, the 355 Boreham Wood to St Albans via Radlett came a bit later on. There were no late night services. Sounds like a lot of services but the regularity left much to be desired. The 311 bus was later changed to the 358.

The only one taxi firm was run by *Harold Stark* in Shenley Road adjacent to All Saints' Church, so there were plenty of bicycles and Shanks's ponies, and with food rationing we were slimmer and fitter.

Eating and Drinking

What did we eat during the War? It is very difficult to remember in detail. Milk, bread and vegetables were always in plentiful supply. I suppose the difficult time was 1941/43 when the German 'U' boat menace was at its height.

Spam, corned beef, dried egg and snoek, which was whale meat, were reasonably available. Most people grew vegetables in their gardens and there were allotments in many areas of Boreham Wood.

Pig clubs were formed and there were regular pig swill collections around the area. Many people also kept chickens and rabbits. There was also a plentiful supply of wild rabbit and pigeons and these could be bought very cheaply in many pub bars, *The Mops and Brooms* being high on the list. So along with rationed items we got by.

The only fruit as such was seasonal; i.e. apples, pears, in the main. Blackberrying was very popular and nettle soup was a favourite with some people. Sweets were rationed and biscuits were a luxury. At times beer was very short and on the odd occasion it was rationed. For a period food coupons were taken in restaurants.

There were very few over-weight people and we all seemed healthier in many ways. Things in general were a lot easier in the country than in the towns and cities. The black market operated more in the built up areas where for a price you could get most things. Clothing coupons, petrol coupons, silk stockings and spirits being high on the list. Cigarettes, especially the popular brands were sometimes in short supply except for Turfs and Tenners. It was through the black market that the *spiv* came into being.

There were a couple of *spivs* in Boreham Wood dealing mostly in cigarettes, the odd bottle of scotch or gin, tinned army rations, petrol and clothing coupons but *"no names no pack drill"* as the saying goes.

The trading usually took place in the gents, and sometimes the ladies toilets in the Crown and Red Lion pubs but they were only amateurs compared to those I came across in Hamburg some years later.

The Blackout

The blackout caused many problems in different ways; breaking the blackout laws could prove very expensive and sometimes earned a prison sentence.

Air aid wardens patrolled the streets and we all became familiar with the shout *"Put that light out!"* sometimes followed by a knock on the door with a warning.

The two usual methods of *'blacking out'* were either by blackout curtains or lightweight frames covered in blackout material.

If arriving home at night, the rooms had to be blacked out before switching on the light. Leaving the house you had to switch off the hall light before opening the front door or the kitchen light before going out the back, and you always slept in dark rooms.

Very few street lights were in use and cars etc. had shades fitted over their headlights. You could even get told off by a warden for lighting a cigarette out in the open. Torches had to be used very carefully.

Buses and trains had very dim lighting. Boreham Wood was very dark at night; to assist the situation double British Summertime was introduced during the War.

Propaganda

We kept abreast of the state of the War through heavily censored newspapers and the carefully scripted news bulletins on the radio which we never missed; the most popular being the nine o'clock news usually read by *Alvar Liddell*.

Many people had war maps pinned up on a wall at home and kept them up to date as much as possible. Letters from the armed forces were heavily censored as were letters from home, especially about bombing damage.

We listened to Lord Haw Haw, (William Joyce), who broadcast propaganda from Germany. He often mentioned the East End of London and once said that instead of dropping bombs on the East End they would drop flea powder and bug wash. He was captured at the end of the War and hanged for treason.

There were many propaganda films shown at the cinema, one of the most popular featured the Wellington Bomber *F for Freddie* in the film, *"One of our Aircraft is Missing"*.

Wartime posters were everywhere; some of the most popular being *"Careless talk costs lives"*, *"Walls have ears"*, *"Be like Dad, keep Mum"*, *"Dig for Victory"* and many more.

Music

Music played a very important part during the War years. In the early days there were the fun songs like, for instance, *"We are going to hang out our washing on the Siegfreid Line"*, *"Run Rabbit Run"*, *"Mairsy Dotes"*, *"Roll out the Barrel"*, *"Peg-o-My-Heart"*, *"Rosaday"*. The most popular dance band throughout the War was the *R.A.F.'s Squadronnaires*.

As the War progressed the more nostalgic songs took over, *"We'll Meet Again"*, *"You'll Never Know"*, *"It Had to be You"*, *"Now is the Hour"* and *"Yours"*.

When the Americans entered the War we had all of the *Glen Miller* hits, the main three being *"In the Mood"*, *"Moonlight Serenade"*, *"Chattanooga Choo Choo"*. As Monty and the Eighth Army made progress in North Africa we had *"Lili Marlene"*.

Bomber Command made Charlie Barnetts *"Skyliner"* their signature tune.

The Yanks arrived in this country and brought with them *"Pistol Packing Momma"*, *"Chocolate Soldier from the USA"*, *"Coming in on a Wing and a Prayer"*, *"Praise the Lord and Pass the Ammunition"*, *Deep in the Heart of Texas"* and many more. They also of course brought *Jitterbugging*.

"Don't Fence Me In" became the signature tune of American prisoner of war aircrews in Germany and the American Army Air Force adopted *"American Patrol"* as their signature tune. *Eroll Flynn* was beating the Japs single handed at the cinema.

At the time of the Normandy landings *"Opus One"* and *"You'd Be So Nice to Come Home To"* were top hits but many did not come home. Ten thousand allied troops died on D-Day.

In the years immediately after the War we had the music from the shows, *"Oklahoma", "Annie Get Your Gun"* being the main two, and Frank Sinatra was becoming popular.

As the years go by, no doubt like many others of my age, music brings back many memories mostly nostalgic. Again, like many more, I would love to do it all again.

Dancing

You could go dancing in Boreham Wood seven nights per week; there were thirteen places to go as follows:-

- The back room at the Crown,
- Clarendon Hall
- Dufay Hall
- Keystone's Canteen
- The Church Hall
- The hall behind the Church Hall
- Upstairs in the Red Lion,
- The Catholic Hall, known locally as the "Sweat Box"
- ABPC Studios
- Smith's Canteen, later Elliott's Canteen
- Hillside School
- The Elstree Way
- The King's Arms.

In consequence many girls from the outlying villages came to Boreham Wood for evening recreation.

We had a very good cinema, ENSA concerts in ABPC Studios, four pubs - *The Wellington, Crown, Red Lion and the Elstree Way,* two late night cafes - *The Spot* and *Mollys,* shows and a pantomime was always put on at the *Dufay Hall* by *Joe Richardson & Co.*

There were plenty of live bands to play at the various dances apart from the local bands usually having a piano, drums, trumpet, and sax or clarinet, guitar and double bass. Most of the Army units had a group of some sort or other; there were also plenty of good records with Glenn Miller to the fore. The usual pattern for dancing was to play three types of dance at a time. For example, three waltzes, three quicksteps, three foxtrots. A Latin American selection would be played always including the Tango. Speciality dances were always incorporated such as the St Bernard's Waltz, Valetta, Palais glide, Hokey-Kokey etc. As time went by the Jitterbug was played more.

Now and again a few American servicemen would make an appearance, but they were no good at ballroom dancing and still can't dance, judging by the films I watched on TV. The girls loved their uniforms.

SOME OF THE WARTIME DANCE VENUES IN BOREHAM WOOD

(photograph- Derek Allen)

Hillside School
Hillside Avenue 2002

(photograph- Elstree & Boreham Wood Museuml)

Keystone's Canteen 1940s

(photograph - Alan Lawrence)

The Clarendon Club (NAAFI)
Glenhaven Avenue 2001

(photograph - Alan Lawrence)

Church Hall
Shenley Road 1960s

(photograph- Derek Allen)

The Crown
Shenley Road

(photograph - Elstree & Boreham Wood Museuml)

The Elstree Way Hotel 1950

From memory there was very little crime as such in the area during the War and there were plenty of Military Police to look after the troops. I can't remember any real incidents except for the odd punch up; usually over girls or when the husband or boy friend came home on leave. Just after the War finished the army camps in Theobald Street were taken over by ex-Polish soldiers and for a year or two there was always friction, especially Saturday nights at the various dance halls between the Poles and the local lads, especially those on weekend leave re the local girls.

Quite a few Poles married local girls and still live in the area.

I remember three in particular who played darts at the Crown: *Louie, Jan* and *Stefan. Louie* became a pal of my Dad and his friends. He was the Camp Commandant and stood no nonsense.

There were quite a few prisoners of war in the area, mostly Italians. They worked mainly on the farms but I do not remember there being any problems with them.

Youth and Sports Organisations

Apart from the Army Cadet Corps who met at Furzehill Road School, there was the Air Training Corps who met in a large hut in Theobald Street, the Girls' Air Training Corps who met at Hillside School, and the Boys' Brigade run by Charlie Sainsbury and who met in the Baptist Hall in Shenley Road.

I think cricket was still played at Elstree.

The senior football club, Boreham Rovers, disbanded at the beginning of the War and the only organised team were the Boreham Wood Swifts, who wore black and white stripes. This was the first time the word *Wood* was used in a football team in the district.

Yachting and general boating activities ceased on the reservoir due to large poles laid in lines across it, chained together and anchored on shore to prevent the possibility of German seaplanes landing in the event of an invasion.

Home of Rest For Horses

One of the well-known attractions of the area apart from the studios was the Home of Rest for Horses, which is now the Farriers Way housing estate. They looked after 50/60 horses and ponies that had been retired and/or ill-treated. None of ours finished up there.

Boreham Wood Men and Women in the Forces

There were many Boreham Wood men and women who served in the Armed Forces during and after the War. The majority were in the Army but quite a few were in the Royal Navy.

Among them I remember *John Gant, Jimmy Dawes, Sean Brady, Tommy Smith, Brian Osborne, George Dagnall, Bill Crossland* and *Ronnie Miller.*

Apart from myself, the only other airmen that I can recall were our next-door neighbour, *Mr Treacher, Johnny Hyde, Cliff Dove* and my brother *Tom.* No doubt there were more, but I am remembering back nearly seventy years.

General

All through the War the whole atmosphere was different, people spoke to each other more freely, you helped each other and shared what you had. We were united in a common aim and never gave a thought that we may have lost the War, we somehow knew we would win. People queued without question, in fact we queued for everything.

Regardless of our politics *Winston Churchill* was our hero and the whole nation listened in to his speeches.

Servicemen were made welcome everywhere regardless of nationality, colour or creed. It was the *'British Bulldog'* spirit and it carried us through.

Newsreels on the War in the cinema were clapped and sometimes cheered, everybody stayed for *The King* at the cinema and at the end of dances. Writing this book I feel proud to have been a very small part of it.

(photograph - Bill O'Neill)

Stables at the Home of Rest for Horses

(photograph - Elstree & Boreham Wood Museuml)

Metropolitan Police Station in Barnet Lane
Converted into a private house, post war

(photograph - Elstree & Boreham Wood Museuml)

Early 1940s advertisement

2.5 SERVICE IN THE R.A.F.

Early in November 1944 Joe Brady, Jackie Bolton and myself, all just turning seventeen, went over to the Army Recruitment Centre in the Drill Hall, Burnt Oak to volunteer for the Army.

They could only offer to recruit us into the Infantry due to the heavy fighting on the Continent following the invasion a few months earlier. I wanted to join the R.E.M.E., the Royal Electrical Mechanical Engineers, or even the Royal Artillery but only cannon fodder was required. I said thanks, but no thanks, Joe and Jackie signed up for the East Surrey Regiment. They were called up in May 1945 and finished up as Sergeants in Greece. I went into the Royal Air Force. In the early days we managed to be home on leave together and throughout our service lives Joe and I corresponded from wherever we were stationed.

The end of the War was an anti-climax. We knew the end was near; Hitler was dead, the Russians were in Berlin. On 7th May we were told that war in Europe would end the next day on 8th May so it was not a spontaneous celebration but celebrate we did.

I spent most of the day playing the piano on a rostrum in the Red Lion car park, (now McDonalds) as there was no room for dancing inside the pub plus the fact that only being seventeen and a half I was not allowed in the pub! But who cared on that day. Although there was peace in Europe there was still a war being fought in the Far East.

I had had my medical at the drill hall in Burnt Oak during February and passed A1, received my calling up papers during April and on Wednesday, 23rd May 1945 reported to R.A.F. Padgate in Lancashire, the furthest I had ever been away from home. The eight days spent there getting kitted out was rough and tough, but after being brought up in the East End, surviving the *Blitz* and living in an Anderson shelter for seven months and three years service in the Army Cadets it was just another hurdle in life, but I do remember hearing some quiet crying during those first few nights.

One of the things being in the Army Cadets did for me when I went into the Air Force was to make it very easy on the initial eight weeks' square bashing etc.

I did my first eight weeks on an American operational airfield in Leiston East Suffolk and our instructors were corporals and sergeants from the R.A.F. Regiment. They had just returned from India and we were their first recruits.

I remember one of the corporals, on our first day as we assembled in full kit and rifles out on one of the runways as a full flight of 120 men, calling out *"All those who have been members of the Army Cadets or Air Training Corps fall out"*. About 35/40 did so. He then called for a *"right marker"*, told the rest of us to fall in in threes, come to attention, shoulder arms, right turn and march off, we then became his squad. The other two instructors just stood there and stared. It became very obvious that we knew more about arms drill etc. than they did.

I found the square bashing very easy having spent nearly four years walking around Boreham Wood six days per week delivering milk or bread.

As I have already stated, I did my basic training on an operational American airfield at Leiston in East Suffolk, it was the home of two Squadrons of Mustangs. After two months of square or *runway* bashing, weapon training and aircraft recognition, of which I had plenty of practice during the preceding five years or so, I was posted along with five others to Morecambe in Lancashire.

When we eventually arrived and reported to the Clarendon Hotel on the front, nobody knew anything about us. The main contingent of R.A.F. personnel having moved a few weeks earlier. The hotel was being refurbished after serving as the headquarters for the area so we were sent to a local café for our meals and put in the cells in the basement for a couple of nights until we were sorted out . We had the best night's sleep since joining up.

We were eventually posted to Heaton Park just outside of Manchester which was a transit camp for airmen returning from overseas, mainly India and the Far East via Liverpool Docks for de-mob.

We were put on permanent staff to await posting for our trade training and went on shifts for general catering and kitchen duties. Being put on permanent staff meant that we had the pick of the girls at the local dances because they knew those in transit were here today and gone tomorrow.

The intakes arrived at various times during the day or night and ours was the first decent food they had seen for some considerable time and were always very appreciative of our service. The main bonus was after nearly six years of war and eight weeks in a training camp we had all the food we could eat, especially our breakfast fry ups.

We had plenty of time off between intakes and we could always pop into the cookhouse for a midnight snack after coming in from a night out.

While there I fell for 'Nancy with the laughing face'. She was a young WAAF.

Just a week or two after arriving the *Atom bomb* brought an end to the War against Japan on 14th August 1945. A large intake had just arrived mainly of walking wounded and long service soldiers some of whom had seen action against the Japanese. The celebrations went on far into the night and most of the following day; where the booze came from I shall never know. Most of them were still in tropical uniform and those that did get out of the camp were treated like conquering heroes in the local pubs. We, as permanent staff, still had our duties to carry out; breakfast was late next morning and there were quite a few missing.

All too soon our postings came through; Melksham in Wiltshire on an eighteen weeks aircraft electricians course.

Having left school at thirteen years of age I found the maths and basic science parts of the course very hard at times so I had to do quite a bit of overtime studying, or in R.A.F. jargon *'genning up'*.

No leave as such, just thirty-six or forty-eight hour passes. It was pay your own fare or hitch hike home. The basic pay was three shillings (15p) per day, two guineas (£2.10) per fortnight.

The course was made that much more interesting because in our intake we had several qualified air crew who had signed on and became redundant at the end of the War and had remustered as electricians. All of them were sergeants and ranged from fighter and bomber pilots, to navigators, wireless ops and air gunners. They had their own quarters and mess so we only mixed on the course, in the local pubs and playing football. Some of the stories they told us about active service were always entertaining especially those from the bomber crews.

Five of them were on my next posting.

Above - Melksham 1945

'Bluey ' Wilkinson and Joe Brady
Home on leave c 1946

First Christmas leave, with Mum
1945

(photographs - Bill O'Neill)

It was while at Melksham that one of the older lads in our intake was getting friendly with one of the local girls and he persuaded the air crew boys to kit him out with one of their tunics so that he could attend a dance at the sergeants' mess, officers invited, knowing the girl in question would be in attendance.

At the dance one of the officer instructors approached him and asked him, *"Do I know you?"* He said *"if not he was the double of one of the lads on the course"*. The *sergeant* replied, *"I think you mean my twin brother."* Not totally convinced the officer replied, *"mm"* and let it go.

A few weeks later at an all ranks dance at the camp the lad in question was at the dance, this time wearing his own tunic with his now girl friend and the same officer, who was also in attendance, walked up and said to him for all to hear, *"Does your brother know you are dating his girl friend?"* and walked away winking at one of the sergeants in passing.

I then had my first Xmas in the Royal Air Force and five days' Xmas leave. On Monday, 24th December 1945 we marched the five miles to Box Station , took the train to Paddington and across London to St. Pancras, then the train to Elstree Station, the journey taking over eight hours arriving home 5.30 pm. Thankfully on our return we had lorries waiting for us.

I survived the course and passed out on Saturday, 19th January 1946 and received a posting to No 218 MU (Maintenance Unit) Colerne, just outside of Bath in Wiltshire as a Group II Aircraft Electrician. 218 MU shared the airfield with No 39 MU which serviced Meteor Jet aircraft.

I was put in the RT & D Section (Receive, Test and Despatch) and all of my work was on Lancasters, Avro Yorks, Mosquitos, Dakota and Lancastrians, which were converted Lancasters and being used for civil airlines.

If my memory is correct they carried nine passengers for day flights and six for overnight flights.

There were at least two hundred and fifty Lancaster bombers parked around the airfield and the vast majority of them were left just as they were after their last operational bombing run.

The least damaged would be serviced and our section would test and despatch them so there was plenty of flying to be done especially on the Lancasters, but not too much on the Yorks or Dakotas. If you were very lucky you had a trip in a Mosquito.

The one pilot I remember was *Pilot Officer Baxter*. On take off he would always sing *"One Meat Ball"* over the intercom, he was also the station's goal keeper and chose to play for our section team against the other sections i.e. Radar – Engines – Airframes – Instruments – Ground Crew and Admin. The derby game was 218 MU v 39 MU.

My very first flight ever was in a Lancaster piloted by Flying Officer Baxter. The date was Monday, 11th March 1946 and the aircraft's No was VL981.

We flew west over the Bristol Channel, turned south over Wales and down to the English Channel crossing Cornwall, turned east and flew along the Channel to the Isle of Wight, turned north- west back to Colerne. Did three touch down circuits, a round trip of approx. 300 miles taking approx. two hours.

We flew at an average height of 7,000 feet so oxygen was not needed.

Lancaster No VL182 taking off from Scampton

Back at RAF Colerne - I took this picture just after landing

Our Crew in Hamburg 1947

(photographs - Bill O'Neill)

For the first half an hour or so I stayed strapped into the seat which is just inside the rear entry door with my eyes glued to the small window beside the seat with my stomach coming up into my mouth every time we hit an air pocket, which was very often. I was eventually persuaded to move forward to the engineer's station and started to carry out the various checks and tests. Gradually over the next few months I got used to the bumpy rides we had, especially over the Irish Sea. When Pilot Officer Baxter spotted some trawlers they were always *dive-bombed* with bomb doors open. We landed at R.A.F. Scampton, the home of the *Dambusters* and on one trip, through fog across the Midlands down to Colerne. In my diary the Lancaster's number was VL182. I would love to do one more trip in a *Lanc.* no doubt as many others would. Every time the Lancaster flies over my back garden at the Southend Air Show, I think you lucky beggars. The nearest I have been to a Lanc. since 1948 was at the Hendon and Duxford Air Museums. I did sit in the mock-up of a Lanc. on the set of The Dambusters in A.B.P.C. Studios, but it didn't smell the same!

One of the tricks we used to get up to when working on Lancasters and running up the engines was to ask one of the new blokes who had joined the section to go to the flight hut and bring some tool or other. To do so he had to jump out of the rear door on the starboard side (about four feet up) and as he did the engines would be revved up and you can guess the rest.

Another little *joke* you had to watch out for was the *electric shock*. When an aircraft is in flight, it picks up static electricity and on landing the Lancaster and no doubt many more types of aircraft at the time discharged the built up static through its rear wheel tyre which had graphite built in. The resistance was measured regularly and on a certain reading the tyre was changed, if it was a borderline case it was sometimes let go and *sometimes* we forgot to tell the other trades when going on a test flight not to be the first to make contact with *Terra Firma* while still touching the aircraft.

The other trades were always looking at ways to getting their own back on the electricians. One of their favourite tricks was when we were running radar cables (Gee and Lorane) through the fuselage of a Mosquito fighter bomber and when we were lying flat out facing aft just behind the pilot's seat they would creep up and pull the dinghy compressed air release, the dinghy being just where we were working so we could not get out until the dinghy was deflated; we were then blamed for catching our foot in the release handle. We soon got wise to this one by disconnecting the cable on the compressed air bottle when working on *Mozzies.* But once your name went on a test flight rota and parachutes were signed for then everybody did their job and you made doubly sure that you checked everything thoroughly before signing the 701 form.

The average crew for a test flight on a Lancaster or a York would be Pilot, Navigator, Radio Op, Flight Engineer, Electrician, Instrument Mechanic, Radar Mechanic.

If you were ever airsick and did not make it to the Elsan bucket at the rear of the aircraft just forward of the rear gunners turret on a Lanc. you cleared it up yourself or paid the riggers five shillings (25p over a day's pay). One of the bonuses we had working on *kitted up* aircraft was after a heavy night in *The Clangers*, our local pub, when a few whiffs of oxygen soon cleared your hangover.

Once you had carried out all of your checks and tests you could roam the aircraft, keeping one hand holding on in case of air pockets and try out all of the various stations; like for instance up in the nose in the bomb aimer's position, the mid upper turret and the rear gunner's turret, and if you were very lucky as I was on a few occasions you could sit on the tip-up seat known as the *'dickey seat'* beside the pilot.

I remember one trip when we had the Padre on board for a flight and we hit more turbulence than usual. He turned several shades of white and my lasting memory of him was leaving the aircraft at the control tower before we went on to dispersal with his dog collar hanging halfway down his chest. We never saw him on board again.

Our local pub in Colerne was the Seven Bells known as *The Clangers*. After every near miss we would celebrate at *The Clangers*. We worked quite long hours and had to fill in flight reports before cycling down to the billets, hoping there was some grub left. The first of my two near misses was at Colerne when we had to land crosswind on the long runway through loss of brake pressure in a York aircraft. The skipper gave us the opportunity to bale out. If there had been a static line to clip your chute on, which released your chute for you, a couple of us might have gone for the experience. I thought I may have done one of two things as we never had any parachute training; either pull the release too soon and finish up on the tailplane or pass out before releasing at all. We were halfway down the runway when a good blast of March wind caught us. We were lying on the floor of the totally empty aircraft, chute under the head, a handkerchief in our mouths holding on to whatever was available. The skipper was keeping us informed over the intercom as to our progress. The wind took us off the runway onto the soft wet ground finishing nose up and all in a heap behind the main bulkhead. The fire engines and ambulance had been driving down the runway as we landed and were on the scene in seconds and before we could start to climb out we were covered in foam. It was freezing cold and raining.

We were then hosed down and taken down to billets for a hot shower, change of clothes and a hot drink with a rum in it; then back up to hangars, took off in another York, did circuits and bumps followed by a good night in *The Clangers*.

While stationed at Colerne I went on *'special sick'* and finished up in St Martin's Hospital in Bath having my appendix removed. There were forty patients in the ward. Thirty-seven civilians, Harry a sailor with an ulcerated leg and John a soldier having been circumcised. He was a comedian in his own right as was Harry, and they had to split us up as I was in danger of bursting my stitches with laughter. Mum and Dad managed to get down once and Mum and brother Tom on another occasion. The lads from the unit could only make the odd Saturday afternoon. I was in there for six weeks.

Hospital visiting was very strict in those days 7.30 – 8.00 pm and only two visitors per patient so if any of the other patients had a spare visitor Harry, John and myself would get them, especially any young daughter visiting, so at times we three sometimes had four around our beds plus plenty of goodies being brought in.

On being discharged it was back to base and a week's sick leave.

Again all too soon, back to Melksham for a Group One Electricians Course; on completion posted to Germany to a unit just outside of Hamburg.

We spent five days at No 5 P.D.C. at Burtonwood getting kitted out, then train to Euston London, then Liverpool St to Harwich, sailed on SS Vienna to The Hook of Holland then by train to Hamburg, lorry to unit, the whole journey taking thirty-six hours. There was still a temporary bridge over the Rhine, the train travelling five miles per hour while crossing. We had arrived at Harwich early evening, fed and watered and marched down to the ship in full kit and rifle plus one blanket. The ship was full with 90% Army and quite a few control commission personnel.

For some reason the R.A.F. was always last on and first off. We were in threes on the dockside and the dozen or so in front of us were called up the very wide gangplank by a Regimental Sergeant Major. I lowered my kit-bag to the ground and propped my rifle up against an adjacent capstan. The next dozen were called forward with me leading half way up the gangplank. I remembered

I had left my rifle behind, I did a quick about turn with the R.S.M. yelling, *"Airman, where are you so and so going to?"* I called back, *"I have forgotten my gun, sir."* Going puce he yelled, *"Gun? Gun? You're not playing so and so Cowboys and Indians now. Rifle, man, rifle."* About mid sixties I sent this story to Readers Digest for the *"Humour in Uniform"* page. If I remember rightly I received £75.00 for it.

In 2008 we sailed from Harwich on a cruise and I went and stood on the exact spot where this incident took place. I wish I had taken a photograph.

Hamburg was in a bit of a state but we had our own service clubs to go to, mainly the Victory Club and the Malcolm Club. The two main night clubs we frequented were Café Fatherland and Café Faun. There were, of course, many other tourist attractions.

We also saw some very good shows at the Garrison Theatre, Danny Kaye being in one of them.

It was in the Victory Club that I met two people from Boreham Wood – Johnny Oliver, brother of Eva who was in the Army and at the time on a night out from the 94th British General Hospital recovering from a motor bike accident, and Les Webster from Essex Road, also in the Army.

There was a *very strict* no fraternisation ban on, which slowly eased off. As time went by things slowly improved especially for the Hamburgers; mainly women and children. Tens of thousands of the German armed forces were still in P.O.W. camps in Russia, North Africa, Canada and England.

There was a thriving black market operating especially in cameras, watches and Nazi memorabilia. I had my swastika flag and SS helmet stolen as well as other bits and pieces but I managed to get a few watches and cameras home plus a very large cuckoo clock, which my Mum kept for quite a few years.

The average weekly pay for the few German men who worked on our base was forty marks per week; at one time a fresh egg cost forty marks.

We were paid in BAFO's (British Air Force of Occupation).

They consisted of notes to the value of two shillings and sixpence (12.1/2p), five shilling notes (25p), ten shilling notes (50p) and one pound notes and we could only spend them in the NAAFI and the service-run clubs.

Although the War had been over for eighteen months or so we still had to be very careful at night, especially going back to camp from a night out in Hamburg. We could never travel alone and always arranged to return in groups of four or five. To go back late at night on your own meant being found on the railway line next morning or in some doorway; our attackers were the remnants of the Hitler Youth who had escaped a P.O.W. camp when the War ended. Their target was always R.A.F. personnel. They thought we were all bomber crews. We were known as 'S..t Tommies'.

The main black market currency was coffee beans and cigarettes; the camp cooks had other currency. You could buy anything including English one and five pound notes. The general rate was approx. five times the buying price in the U.K. for quite a while. Our post to and from the U.K. was free being marked *"On active service".*

Most of the parcels we received contained coffee beans. We could buy cigarettes in the NAAFI's.

Entrance and
Guard House

Fun in the
NAAFI

Winner
takes all

Hamburg Germany 1947

(photographs - Bill O'Neill)

Having a break Germany 1947

Tea Break in Overalls

BOW BELLS TO BOREHAMWOOD

I then had my first Christmas in Germany. Things were still in a bit of a mess. I suppose we did have some time off but for some reason or other I do not remember too much about it and my diary of the time does not tell me too much. I don't think the Germans did too much celebrating. My first leave since my fourteen day embarkation leave was not due until February so I had to wait for a late Xmas dinner with Mum's cooking plus a few pints of *Main Line* in the Crown.

In November of 1947 we were all on parade for the march through Hamburg to celebrate the Royal Wedding of Princess Elizabeth.

Apart from working on the aircraft, as electricians we also carried out re-wiring of trucks, small lorries and armoured cars for No 5 MTBD (Motor Transport Base Depot), an adjacent unit. We also did our turn of duty electrician overnight, checking the charging of the trolley accumulators used for starting up aircraft, known as trolley Acc's. It was a twelve hour shift 8.00 pm – 8.00 am. We operated from the guard house and the workshop buildings and airfields were patrolled by recruited displaced persons (D.P's) awaiting repatriation. They were mostly Polish. They were issued with navy blue uniforms and berets with the red Hamburg cross. They were also armed and trigger happy.

Every two hours or so we would do our checks on the equipment using bicycles to get around. To let them know we were coming we would whistle *"Rule Britannia"*. Try that with a dry mouth. After a couple of near misses their rifles were taken away and they were given dogs with strict instructions to keep them on long leads.

We also did twelve hour overnight guard duty, two hours on four hours off up at the airfield where we stood in the sentry box just outside of the entrance to the guard house. One very cold January night I was on guard duty, greatcoat collar up, Balaclava helmet on under my "tin" hat, my backside just resting on the plank seat inside the sentry box leaning slightly forward on my rifle, very light snow falling, almost nodding off when I was conscious of someone coming towards me. I then saw that he was holding a revolver and speaking to me in German. I raised my rifle towards him, called out *"Halten!"* then shouted *"Call out the guard!"*. Within seconds the Sergeant of the Guard and one of the other lads came running out of the guard house and grabbed the man disarming him. We took him into the guard house, he was more scared than we were. The weapon was a service revolver he had found and had come to hand it in. Four bullets had been fired with still two to go. It was later discovered that the gun had been used in an armed robbery on a nightclub in Hamburg. The MP's were called and he was taken away with the gun. Although I was only half way through my 2 hour shift I asked the Sergeant if I could go to the loo...

Mentioning the D.P's being given uniforms reminded me of the first weekend they wore them; they went en masse into Hamburg to continue the War against the Germans. Luckily they were not armed. Several local units including ours were called upon to man armoured cars and go to Hamburg on stand by. We were armed with batons but never had to use them.

We got to know some of the *Polish* lads and they often invited us to their base which was in Berlinator, a suburb just outside of Hamburg. On the occasions I visited I never remembered going back to camp. The oxygen bottles were well used next morning. They always put on a good spread for us and the one thing I always remember about it was that there seemed to be beetroot with everything. It was also my very first introduction to *Vodka* or as they called it *Wodka*.

Although stationed in Germany my home base was still 218 MU Colerne, and very rarely did we get the opportunity to pop home when dropping off or picking up aircraft, mainly Dakotas and Avro Yorks. There were also a few casualties.

Home on leave with Aunt Flo Dyer
and twins Sylvia and Linda

Ollie with the ginger nurse
from the Channel Islands
at a camp dance.

Inspection before marching through Hamburg to celebrate the wedding of
Princess Elizabeth. I am last on the right of third row, first section
November 1947

(photographs - Bill O'Neill)

Officers and Sergeants on their way to serve lunch

Lunch

Merry Christmas!

Being waited on by the officers - Christmas in Germany 1947

My second near miss was in Germany, landing in a Lancaster when the port undercarriage collapsed on landing without warning. I was sitting on a double bench seat, which was not usual in Lancs, about halfway down the fuselage just aft of the Radome.

The aircraft slewed off the main runway across the airfield, over the perimeter track and into the perimeter fence taking a great chunk with it. I don't suppose the whole incident took more than ten seconds. The skipper had cut the engines and there seemed to be complete silence then voices asking who was okay. I had received a knock on the head and on bracing myself I had my right foot trapped between the bench I had been sitting on and the Radome, which was a large circular unit about two feet high with a cover on top that housed the radar.

The aircraft was nose up at an angle in a small ditch just outside of the perimeter fence. By now the rescue services had arrived. Luckily no one had been right up the front in the bomb aimer's position and the only casualties were a radar mechanic with a broken arm and me with a bump on my head and a very sore right ankle after they had cut my boot off, but I still managed to celebrate that night in the camp NAAFI at tuppence a pint.

Many years later whenever I had a high temperature through a very heavy cold or the 'flu I was back in that aircraft with my foot trapped asking my wife to release me. She soon learnt to hold my foot, just pull and tell me the boot was off. I would be okay then. On one or two occasions my two children Chris and Amanda would ask, *"Can we come in and watch you get Daddy's boot off?!*

When we did get leave we came home by train and ship.

The troopships I remember were the Empire Wandsbeck, Empire Parkeston, Vienna and Georgic. The Empire Wandsbeck was later re-named the Empire Windrush and was used to bring hundreds if not thousands of immigrants from the West Indies. It caught fire and sank in 1954.

I spent my second Christmas in Germany and over the Xmas we had three days off and transport was laid on to attend Midnight Mass in Hamburg. On Xmas Day, by tradition, other ranks had their Xmas dinner served by the officers who had their tunics turned inside out and were wearing German helmets etc. On Boxing Day morning I remember waking up, or was it coming back from the dead, and slowly looking around and saw that I was still dressed and lying on the floor on a mattress under a blanket with a figure all in white standing over me. I thought, *"Was this my guardian angel?"* On looking further around I saw empty beer and wine bottles and a plate with a turkey carcass on it; a vague memory came back of spending the late evening in the cook's billet and the figure in white was *Jock,* one of the cooks up and dressed for breakfast duty. I then remembered that I was due to play football in a charity match against a local German team, eleven a.m. kick-off. Back to my own billet, shave and shower, quick breakfast, grabbed my kit, last one on the lorry still half cut. I remember very little about the game. Just about made the sick parade next day, finished up in the 94th British General Hospital, Hamburg, spent New Year's Eve drinking cocoa with a little ginger nurse from the Channel Islands. Discharged 3rd January the M.O. saying that he booked me in with 'flu but told me to stay off the *unknown* hard stuff while in Germany. Thank you, sir.

Things had been and were very hectic owing to the continued problems being encountered getting in and out of Berlin due to the Russians trying to blockade the city. Obviously the build up to the Berlin Airlift had been going on for some time hence the increase of traffic in the larger aircraft between the U.K. and the airfields in the Hamburg area in particular, with all unnecessary gear being stripped from the aircraft to carry everything from coal to eggs down the Berlin Corridor.

On armoured car duty Hamburg 1947

There were casualties

(photographs - Bill O'Neill)

On arrival back from my last leave in mid February 1948 the whole atmosphere was different, security had tightened and my demob number, 71, was getting near to the top of the list. Another short course in Berlin and I was on one of the last trains from Berlin to Hamburg that had not been held up by the Russkis.

Pressure was put on me and one or two others to sign on for a two or five year period by the Section Leader, *Wing Commander Bird*, known of course as *Dicky*, but after giving some serious thought I decided to go for demob.

After a very hectic couple of months plus a *few* demob parties, I left on the 6 am train from Hamburg on Saturday, 24th April 1948. It was Cup Final day, Manchester United beating Blackpool 3-2. Arrived at Viceroy Court, Regents Park early on the Sunday afternoon. Late train to Kirkham 101 P.D.C. Next morning Monday, 26th April demobbed. Midnight train from Preston arriving in Boreham Wood 9.30 am Tuesday, 27th April with my civvy suit, raincoat and Trilby hat, £78.00 gratuity and eighteen weeks paid leave with mixed feelings and already missing the lads.

The Berlin airlift started in earnest June 1948.

Home in a changed Boreham Wood, but *"What do I do now?"*

Dad in my de-mob gear
Rock Studios in the background

(photograph - Bill O'Neill)

No doubt like thousands more I had very few civilian clothes, I had a two piece suit which I had made in Germany, thanks to coffee beans. I also had the demob suit which fitted where it touched. Dad took a fancy to my demob raincoat so over to *'Bricks'* gents outfitters in Burnt Oak Broadway for shirts etc.

Again like many more we stayed in uniform for a few weeks after demob feeling more comfortable and knowing that when we eventually put it away for good it would be the end of an era.

For the first week or two, at times you felt very lonely and missing the banter of the billets and having to get used to sitting on a chair when you came in instead of flopping out on your bed. Spending quite a bit of time in the Crown and Red Lion helped the gratuity money to run out. At times the signing on option seemed attractive.

Outside the Red Lion Public House Boreham Wood c1949
Monty Tomblin   Me   Bill Sambridge   Bobby Osborne (Ozzie)
Les Kelly   Cliff Dove

(photograph - Bill O'Neill)

I came home on my last fourteen day U.K. leave from Germany in February 1948 and managed to get a very large Bavarian cuckoo clock for Mum. It just about fitted my kit-bag and the clock took pride of place in Clarendon Road; the grandchildren when they came along loved it and nearly wore its *cuckoo* out.

Simon, brother Tom's youngest, called Jean's Mum *Nanny Pippi* after the budgie she had. To balance things up he called my Mum *Nanny Cuckoo Linda*. Mum used to say, *"Anybody listening to him will think I am not all there!"* One day when Dad was winding the clock up he pulled too hard on the chain holding the weight, it fell off the wall and hit him on the head. The clock never quite *cuckooed* after that.

The following is an article I wrote for an annual newsletter for one of the organisations I belong to.

Cruising on the Saga Ruby (we prefer the Rose) during 2006 we had a day long stopover in Kiel after transiting the canal and I took the opportunity of going down to Hamburg to see where I was stationed in the Royal Air Force 1946-48.

All aboard time was 4.30 pm so I had a very tight schedule. Kiel Railway Station was in walking distance of where we were moored and I missed the 9.20 am train by minutes, having trouble in sorting a ticket out (£30.00 return) so I hung about and caught the 10.20 am which arrived at

Hamburg Central at 12.00 noon. The last time I arrived there was in February 1948 after going back from U.K. leave and a lorry was waiting for me then.

The journey was from Liverpool Street to Harwich then by ship to the Hook of Holland, then a sixteen-hour journey by train to Hamburg. It used to take several minutes to cross the Rhine on the repaired bridge, the train moving at a snail's pace.

I walked out of the station, which by now had all of its roof on! The cobbled section of road where the lorries used to park was still there.

I then managed to find somebody who could understand my German and speak some English who then escorted me to the underground platform for the second leg of my *pilgrimage* i.e. the local train to Ochzensoll where the barracks and airfield were, a journey of 35 minutes. The underground part was only 3-4 stations, then above ground, going through all of the then familiar names brought back many memories.

Back then Ochzensoll was at the end of the line but it now carries on for several miles. I arrived about 12.45 pm and walking up the steps again brought back memories of coming back from a night out in Hamburg, helping each other up the steps and the short distance to the camp entrance.

All I could recognise was the station, the railway sidings where all our supplies of coal came into and which we had to guard in the very cold winters, and one building that used to be a café bar and now a *McDonalds.*

The road from the barracks to that where the airfield and workshops were passed the station. When we marched to and from the airfield it had only forces traffic on it, but it is now a main road.

I had taken some photographs of the barracks with me and stopped a couple of older people and again with my German managed to ascertain that the camp, which had been a small arms factory, had long gone as had the airfield.

When I showed one elderly lady the photographs she said *"Ja, the Luftwaffe"*. I said *"Nein, the R.A.F.".* She only hit me once!

I was by now keeping a close eye on the time as there was only one train from Hamburg Central that could get me back to Kiel in time – the 2.30 pm due in Kiel 4.10 pm.

I had one more look around but there was nothing that really reminded me in detail, after all a lot has happened in sixty years.

I travelled back to Hamburg alighting at Stephensplatz, two stops before the main line station to see what I could remember about the area we used to visit at night and week-end leave, here I had more luck. The Opera House was still there as was the building that used to be the Victory Club. The inner Alster still looked the same and, like London, it was difficult to tell what was left of the old (not much when I was there) and what is now new. I did not have time to find out if the Winklestrasse was still there!

I arrived back at Hamburg Central Station about 2.10 pm, managed to get a seat on the main line train after checking several times that I was on the right train. Arrived back in Kiel a few minutes late and walked up the gangplank at 4.25 pm.

Should you go back? I am very pleased that I did, I had always wanted to. I didn't quite know what to expect but I have now visited all of the R.A.F. units I served on. The training camp at Melksham and the operational units at Leiston, East Suffolk and Colerne in Wiltshire. I have promised myself a trip to Manchester to see if the lake and tunnel are still in Heaton Park. It was about a ten minute walk from our billets in what was known as consumption valley to the kitchens and mess hall where we worked. It was right in the middle of summer and walking through the trees and around the lake and through the tunnel at five o'clock in the morning was something I have always remembered.

Colerne was the only unit where I worked alongside WAAFS and mixed with them in normal camp life. Now and again one of them would sneak on a Lanc. for a short trip. They always joined in any celebration in the *Clangers*. In our particular group there were three WAAFS and five airmen and if we had had a good result on the black market in Germany we would go for a meal in the *Grapes or Grapevine*, a local pub-restaurant and at the time the *poshest* restaurant and the only restaurant I had been in. I think that applied to most of us.

As the youngest in the gang I was well looked after especially after showing one of the corporals how to snare rabbits having learnt the art when hopping. We sold a few to the pub.

Before joining up I had acquired a very powerful slug gun and smuggled it back to camp having noticed that *Jugged Hare* was one of the dearest items on the restaurant's menu and there are always plenty of hares on airfields. We never did manage to hit one. I sold the air rifle to a local for £3.00 having lost heavily at '*shoot pontoon*', the aircrew card game, just prior to going on leave before posting back to Melksham for the group one course.

There were lots of superstitions in the forces especially among air crew during the War. I had one during the *Blitz*. Whenever I heard the song *"The Singing Hills"* on the radio there always seemed to be an air raid more heavy than usual and if it came on I would turn it off or leave the room.

I remember one of the redundant air crew lads telling me that he never boarded an aircraft without patting the side of the fuselage twice before boarding and saying to himself *"Thank you"*. In consequence from my very first trip in March 1946 I did this and have done so ever since.

I clearly remember my first flight on a commercial airliner in 1961 from London airport to Nutts Corner, Belfast. It was on a Vickers Viscount. I was working for BSP Industries in Maxwell Road at the time and on my first visit of many to Short and Harlands, Queens Island, Belfast, working on the *Belfast*, a large four engined transport plane for the R.A.F. I sat on the aisle seat, first row aft of the galley. On take off I found myself gripping the arm rests and sweating and then lighting up as soon as the smoking sign went on.

The stewardess noticed that I was *disturbed* and brought me a glass of water. After a few minutes the aircraft straightened out into the smoothest ride I had ever had. I then realised what the problem was. It was the first time I had ever flown without a parachute and not being a part of what was going on and realising that if anything went wrong there was no way you could get out. Later on when jets came into service and flying at 30,000 feet plus it was unreal and detached with no sense of speed from take off to touch down, plus being a lot quieter and warmer. Mentioning warmer, we were always scrounging from the WAAFS their old service issue stockings when flying in the winter. They soon got wise to the thriving black market in Germany especially in cocktail watches and cameras so strong bartering went on when we returned to base. We were never questioned when returning but to make sure we used to hide bits and pieces in the aircraft for a day or so just to be sure. I don't ever remember seeing a service policeman at dispersal, and during the winter months they very rarely came out of the guardroom.

Being able to knock a tune out on a piano was certainly a bonus in the forces. In those days all pubs had a piano, also most houses. Apart from earning a few bob the pints used to line up on the piano and more often than not you were invited back to a party and if one or two of the lads could give a song then that was a bonus.

We used to share the pints and I would give them twenty five percent of the hat and/or what the guv'nor of the pub donated. In fact during the first few years of marriage I played the piano Friday and Saturday evenings in the Red Lion for three pounds plus the box. This paid for my first car bought in 1953, a 1933 Austin Seven (JJ8149). It cost fifty pounds and enabled me to attend evening classes in Barnet, Hendon and Watford. The car had to be picked up from Totteridge and as I had not yet passed my test. Joe Brady came with me to drive it home. For some reason or other there was a spare steering wheel in the car; you can guess the rest. The sight of a very small Austin Seven being driven by two people looking quite serious caused quite a few double takes on our way home. Joe and I had many laughs about that incident and we still do.

When I informed Mum and Dad in December 1944 that I had volunteered to join the Royal Air Force it was received with mixed feelings. The War was still being fought in Europe and in the Far East against the Japanese, with heavy losses all round and with no real end in sight.

I argued that if I waited until I was called up it was a dead cert that it would be for the Army especially with over three years service in the Army Cadets and War Certificate 'A' to my name. I think they saw the point and from the trade training I received and the service life I had, plus a smarter uniform, I made the right choice. Once I had settled in I was for the first time in my life getting three meals a day on a regular basis, a bed to myself, no trudging round in all weathers' for a time seven days per week, and having to put the horses first regardless of the weather, never getting soaked through and putting damp clothes on in the mornings, plus getting twice my weekly wage and when home on leave a nicely pressed tunic, starched collar and tie plus Brylcreem. So what more could you want? The one thing I did miss when I got demobbed and was my greatcoat.

I mentioned on the previous page that I worked for B.S.P. Industries after leaving Keystones. During the seven years I worked there I received a wealth of experience through working on various projects. Thinking about this period reminds me of when the offices were completed and the fire station was built in front of them. Mr *Ivor Bailey*, the guv'nor, offered a prize for the best name for the road. The winner was *Decimal Place*. When it went to the Fire Brigade for approval, they replied *"As we are at the front we suggest it be called Fire Place"*. The local council stepped in and I haven't a clue where Maxwell Road came from.

It took some time to get away from aircraft; apart from doing several trips to Belfast I was for a while during the fifties out on site at Handley Page, Park Street for B.S.P. working on the *Victor Bomber* and the *Hastings* transport aircraft.

2.6 DE-MOB AND KEYSTONES

I spent the best part of my service life in Germany and was demobbed April 1948; I had eighteen weeks and three days leave to come.

Although I had been home on leave during the period I was serving I had not taken much notice of what was happening in and around Boreham Wood. The Crown and Red Lion were still there as were most of the dance halls and at the time that was all that mattered.

Building had begun early 1946 on the housing estates both north and south of the *'village'* as it was called then and still is by a few of the locals. The gaps along Shenley Road between the shops were being filled, the prefabs had gone up in Eldon Avenue and the Hartforde Road area was well advanced and for the next ten years or so building never stopped.

Work was not easy to find at this time. I had completed two eighteen week courses plus one six week advanced course on electrics in the Air Force but could not find any suitable work.

I tried house wiring on the estates that were being built but houses do not have electrically operated gun turrets, identification lighting or engineers panels built in or radar domes or automatic bomb selectors in their living rooms.

Joe Brady was demobbed about the same time as me so we spent a lot of time playing darts at the Crown and were always together; neither of us had girl friends at the time. We were just enjoying the freedom of peace and service life since 1939.

Guy Fawkes Night 5th November 1948 fell on a Friday. Joe Brady and I met at our usual time of 7.30 pm to go to The Crown for our usual few pints and a game of darts. The only difference on that particular night was that we had tickets for a dance at Shenley Hospital. We had a good run on the dartboard and had to run to catch the last 358 bus to Shenley (10.30 pm) at the stop at the Central Garage, in fact the conductor saw us running and held the bus up for us.

At 12.30 am when the dance finished Joe informed me that he was walking a girl home and would I see her friend, Marge Cook, home; being a gentleman I obliged. We reached home after our walk from Shenley about 2.30 am. I remember that I had worn a new pair of shoes and had removed them at the bottom of Cowley Hill.

Saying goodnight to *Joe* at the bottom of Cardinal Avenue I said, *"Meet you tomorrow at twelve o'clock to go to The Crown"*. He replied, *"No, I won't be there. I have got a date."* I said, *"Not the one with the eye patch and the velvet dress."* *"Yes"* he said, *"that's the one"*. The girl was *Cissie Parkins* who *Joe* eventually married. The eye patch was covering a black eye caused by a firework earlier in the evening. For the next few weeks I hated *Cissie* for nicking my best mate but we eventually became good friends and we still are.

As I said in the introduction of this book *Cissie* and my wife to be had been friends since infant school. As it turned out Joe only beat me to the courting stage of life by a few weeks.

I had during my time in the forces and the first few months of demob taken a few girls out. *Eve Oliver, Joan Barnes, Gloria Turner* and *Dot Miller* in particular and had kept in touch with *Diana McEvoy* throughout my service life. *Diana* was a very good friend and we wrote regularly.

I also had a week in Rhyl, North Wales staying with my best mate *Eric Oliver, Ollie,* who was home on leave. He stayed on in Germany as a regular.

Joe's father, *Pat Brady*, had been working in the fully fashioned stocking department of Keystone Knitting Mills long before the War along with many others in Boreham Wood and the surrounding district and he arranged for us to get onto their trainee programme. Although Nylon had been used for stocking manufacture in the States it was only just arriving in the U.K. Nylon by the way is a made up word; New York – London taken from the two cities where it was invented. Keystones had bought twenty or so second hand Nylon knitting machines from the States to add to their twenty or so machines that were using Lisle and Artificial Silk, which on a two shift system needed eighty or so operators.

The trainee starting wage was £5.00 for a forty-hour week and for a six to ten week training period. Income Tax was five shillings per week, National Insurance four and eleven pence, so take home pay was four pounds ten shillings and a penny. The carrot was the average wage that could be earned once you had your own machine and went into the two shift system 6 am – 3 pm and 3 pm – 12 pm, which was eighteen pounds per week and which was a great deal of money then.

When I had my first job on the drawing board in 1954 my weekly wage was eight pounds ten shillings.

Later, when I came out of the Air Force I was receiving seven shillings and sixpence a day trade pay and one shilling and sixpence a day flying pay, total nine shillings (45 pence) giving a three pound three shilling a week wage, all found, plus cheap cigarette allowance and cheap beer, especially in Germany so like many others I became worse off. We had to contribute at home, buy new clothes etc. so it was a struggle and we were always broke on Mondays.

Our first job as trainees was to clean oil off all of the parts of the machines that had arrived from the States prior to the fitters assembling them.

Most of the trainees were local lads just coming out of the forces, our instructors were two experienced knitters, *Noel Ramsey* and *Barney Jacks* with *Pat Brady* Senior helping out.

Some of the trainees I remember working with

Joe Brady	Johnny Oliver	Frankie Arnott	Albert Drummond
Dennis Bliss	Eric Potts	Evan Hallas	Stan Smith
Joe Huggan	Ray Eales	Jim Read	Ron Allridge
Frank Goodwin	Jack Pemberton	Vic Hunt	Les Farnham
John Juett	John McEvoy	Dennis Reeves	
Stan Hextall	Pat McEvoy	Tony Tulip	

Senior knitters still working there who had worked there before and some during the War

George Wilkie	Jackie Cocharan	Harry Needham	Tom Bullock
Tom Parsons	Alex Crosby	Alf Corner	Jack Bullock
Jack Gardener	Johnny Slane	Nick Anderson	Jack Turner
Ralph Gardener	Joe Kelly	Georgie Gaul	Joe Huggan Snr
Bob Sharkey	Gordon Hind	Pat Brady	Mick Redican
Andy Sharkey	Albert Clark	Dick Oliver	Jack Thornicroft
Eddie Higgins			

Keystones had several types of knitting machine.

Number Used	Type of knitting machine
4	Topping machines - footers
8	Completes which knitted the whole stocking
10	Readings - leggers - which came from the States
2	Schuberts - very old leggers
about 12	Kalios -leggers

They had twenty four heads and were about twenty feet long, and could be operated along that length at any point by a rod. You were on your feet almost continually during your shift. Apart from watching all twenty-four stockings being knitted you had to keep your eye on the bobbins so that you changed them in time so as not to lose a stocking. The knitting shed was very hot and noisy with the machines going continually from 6 am until midnight. If some of the knitters had the chance for several minutes afterwards they could get one more bundle off. The average twenty-four stocking bundle was one dozen per shift.

We started off with the welt, the stocking top, then stopped the machine to fold them over then knitted down to the start of the heel. They were then checked and given to the four topping machines to finish off before going to the dyeing and seaming departments.

Each topping machine, again twenty four heads long, was operated by a man and a boy.

George Read	Eric Brazier,	David Langley	Alan Paley,
Eric Chambers	John Atkins.		

Among the toppers were

Thelma Buckenham	Cissy Parkins	Gladys Kelloway	Dot Langley
Helen Moss	Olive Clark	Audrey Clark	Margaret Dobson
Eileen Crosby	Ivy Laydon	Eileen Agombar	Norah Laydon
Dot Murdoch	Nora Chandler	Jean Brown	Ivy Mitchell
Molly Gilchrist	Priscilla Bagnall		

The toppers worked two shifts 6 – 2 pm and 2 – 10 pm. The leggers 6 – 3 pm and 3 – 12 pm. The department head was Mr Atwell. The mechanics were his two sons Dennis and Norman, who both played cricket for Elstree, and Nobby Clark.

The toppers' forelady was Gladys Baker and the quantity checker was Fred ? Among the permanent cleaners were Jim Stoneman, Tommy Hoy, for a time Mick Webb and big Dave from Shenley and Mr Smith, Stan Smith's father.

There were of course a few romances between the trainees and the toppers, which resulted in a few marriages namely, Joe Brady and Cissy Parkins, Bill O'Neill and Thelma Buckenham, Joe Huggun and Dot Murdoch, George Read Jnr and Audrey Clark, Ray Eales and Ivy Laydon, Barry Armour, a knitter, married Olive Clark and Eddie Higgins married Pricilla Bagnall.

By early 1949 we were all classed as knitters with most of the ex-trainees still working on Lisle and Art Silk whilst the big money was earned on the Nylon. For a period we went onto three shifts 6 – 2 pm, 2 – 10 pm and 10 – 6 am. When we changed shifts my then wife to be and I were sometimes on opposite shifts for long periods. I would meet her off her 2 – 10 pm shift and be walking home meeting some of the 3 pm – 12 pm shift going home, I never made my quota on early shift.

There was also a seamless department upstairs in Keystone and among those who worked there were Bob Langley, Wilf Paley, Reg Fitzhugh. There was also a very large lingerie department.

Topping Machine Area 1941

Legger Machine Area
Harold Attewell, centre, ran the fully fashioned department with his sons
Dennis, left, and Norman, right

(photographs - Elstree & Boreham Wood Museuml)

I suppose the total workforce at the time was over the two hundred mark. It all came to an end mid 1952 when all of the ex-trainees were made redundant after four years including all of the topping department. So my wife to be and myself were out of work two months before our wedding in August 1952 and within a short time of the first redundancies the whole of the fully fashioned department had closed down. Tights were coming into fashion!

There are obviously names I have not included, purely because I cannot remember and there are quite a few faces I cannot put a name to, this applies right through the write-up.

Looking back I suppose leaving Keystones was a major turning point in my life, shift work was never my cup of tea but like many others, and I would guess the majority who worked in the fully fashioned department, the money we earned was the prime factor.

In the book that I wrote in 2005 about the *History* of *Boreham Wood Football Club* I touched on this because if I had continued on shift work I would not have been able to get involved with the club as I did, and I would not have been able to go to evening classes for the seven years that I did after leaving Keystones, which enabled me to take up where I had left off with my time spent on various courses in the Air Force and eventually run my own businesses etc.

Keystone Girls 1950
Outing to Southend

Dot Murdoch Thelma Buckenham
Gladys Calloway and Jean Brown

Mum and Dad   1961

(photographs - Bill O'Neill)

2.7   FINAL THOUGHTS

I considered myself lucky to be living in Boreham Wood during the War years. Although we could hear and at times see the continual bombing of London, there were very few direct hits on Boreham Wood. The nearest *Doodlebug* fell just behind the houses in Tennison Avenue and did quite a bit of damage. The next nearest was halfway down Theobald Street in a field killing a few cows.

The nearest V2 rocket fell at South Mymms. I was in the Studio Cinema at the time and small pieces of ceiling and clouds of dust fell down, but the film carried on.

Quite often during a raid you would hear the odd German aeroplane and a few V1s pass over. You also heard the explosions of the V1s and V2s that fell north of London.

There is one date that sticks out in my mind and that was Saturday, 10th May 1941, almost eight months to the day since the *Blitz* had started; it turned out to be the last major air raid of the War. We had only been in Boreham Wood for about three weeks and were still living at Brownlow Road where the upstairs living room faced south. Having no air raid shelter to go to we stayed where we were. We turned the lights out and opened the curtains where we could see the red glow in the sky over London.

Records show that the raid lasted for over eight hours. 700 tons of high explosives and 100,000 incendiaries were dropped by 550 German aircraft in two waves. Conditions were perfect, a full "Bombers' moon" and the Thames at low tide with the attack concentrating on the East End and the docks. Dad was still in Becontree along with many of our relatives and friends plus those still living on Millwall. There were a few tears.

Whereas during the Battle of Britain I could tell the difference between Spitfires and Hurricanes by sight and sound and could recognise most of the German aircraft, we were now as lads giving each other recognition tests on the various Allied aircraft. My number one mate in this was Joe Parkins who lived in Whitehouse Avenue and together we made many Balsa Wood model aircraft.

At night we would watch the Lancasters, Halifaxes and Stirling bombers going out and early morning watch them return with many gaps in the formations.

Mid-morning the American squadrons of Fortresses, Bostons and Liberators aircraft would fly out and return late afternoon again with large gaps in their formation. The Bostons always seemed to fly lower than the Fortresses and often damage could be seen.

On D-Day squadrons of black and white striped winged aircraft and gliders flew south in an almost continual stream and for several weeks before and after D-Day the railway line had almost continual army traffic on it.

Boreham Wood was then really a large village with everybody knowing almost everybody else. I believe the residential population at the time including Well End and Green Street and possibly Shenley was seven thousand. With all of the farms around, milk, eggs etc. were never a problem or the odd rabbit or piece of pork.

As I have mentioned in the write-up there was plenty of entertainment and the Studio Cinema was open seven days per week, two and sometimes three shows per day with the programme change Monday, Tuesday, Wednesday/Thursday, Friday, Saturday/Sunday. So you could go three times per week as most people did.

Another place we used to visit quite often was the roller skating rink in Cricklewood on the Edgware Road. It was an easy trip by steam train from Elstree Station.

Bill   John Cole   Les Kelly   Jim Dawes

I made some very good friends in Boreham Wood and I am still in touch with many of them, unfortunately I do not have any long-standing school friends. I left them behind in 1940 and many of them did not survive the bombing and never attending school in Boreham Wood I had to start from scratch.

I enjoyed living in Boreham Wood up to and around the mid eighties when it all really began to change, but I still feel the halcyon days from my point of view were from 1942 to around 1975.

With regards Boreham Wood being shown as two words, that's how it began. It was the buses sometime in the late seventies that started to show it as one word and businesses started to follow suit. Deacons Hill, Allum Lane and all that area suddenly became *Elstree* I shall never know why. Elstree to my mind starts at the Watling Street end of Allum Lane and half way along Barnet Lane. The next thing will be the lower end of Theobald Street becoming known as Radlett.

The Film Studios started using *Elstree* as their address and still like to be known as *The Elstree Studios.* The whole area has a WD6 postcode.

As someone recently said to me:

The Film Studios are in Elstree, but Big Brother and Eastenders are made in Borehamwood (one word!)

One observation I would make about the Film Studios is that during the late forties and through the fifties when all of the studios were busy it was quite common to see film stars in make up and sometimes in costume using the shops and eating places in Boreham Wood, especially the Grosvenor Restaurant, because in those days there were no restaurant facilities inside the studios. Nobody would take the slightest notice of them but if they were attending a premiere or similar in London in the evening they would be mobbed.

I still have a tie I won from *Erol Flynn* by beating him at darts in the *Red Lion* saloon bar when he was filming at *ABPC Studios*.

If my memory is correct, the film was *"The Master of Ballantrae"*.

Looking at the number of *shops* i.e. shops where you could go in and buy something, Boreham Wood was far better off during and for a few years after the War than it is now. Take the *service* shops out of Shenley Road and what is left? By service shops I mean banks, building societies, estate agents, opticians, undertakers, restaurants and cafes.

In the years I am writing about Boreham Wood was like a village, some of the older residents still refer to it that way i.e. *"Going down the village"*. It was totally surrounded by countryside but only eleven miles from Central London.

Oh happy days and happy memories!

During the writing of this book I realised that the Blitz experience and my service in the Royal Air Force was hardly thought about or for that matter talked about for a very long time after. It is only in recent years that nostalgic memories have become more vivid.

Having spoken to many who have war time memories they have said the same, especially those who saw real action. Tears can come very easily on certain memories, some music and some programmes on T.V. about the War years in particular. No doubt we have all thought that we wish we had taken more notice of certain happenings at the time and looking back you ask yourself "Did that really happen?" At the time of writing this book 2008/09 I am reliving many wartime memories through my grandson George 7/8 years of age having told him about several instances in this book. He knows several of the stories off by heart and never gets tired of listening to them. I sincerely hope that he never has to live through any of the wartime ones.

There came one worrying, exciting, apprehensive incident in 1951 at the time of the Korean War. I had been courting Thelma Buckenham for nearly three years and plans were laid for marriage during 1952, which happened.

I received notification of being called back into the Air Force as a "Z" reservist. We became known as "Zed Men". Along with the orders came a travel warrant to report to R.A.F. Hendon on five days notice, as and when. From then on the progress of the Korean War was watched with mixed feelings.

Fortunately a solution was found and peace was declared; although relieved at not possibly having to go to Korea, I rather fancied the thought of getting married in uniform. It would have saved a few quid on a suit!

The time I have written about in particular I can only describe as follows:-

- It was the best of times.

- It was the worst of times.

- It was the Second World War.

I wonder what the thoughts would be today of those that made the supreme sacrifice during the War years towards some areas of society that disregard those that survived?

I hope you have enjoyed reading this book and that it has brought back a few memories.

Memories are very important, treasure them because memories are forever.

During the writing of this book I have visited Elstree and Boreham Wood Museum on a number of occasions and I have come to realise the time and dedication given by the volunteers who work there. They have gathered, in a very small space, a comprehensive history of the area and regularly put on new displays. I would like to thank Alan and David for their guidance during the compilation of this work and Ann and Deborah for their proofreading and hospitality.

Bill O'Neill

EPILOGUE

The decision to move away from Boreham Wood was not taken easily. The grim reaper had been busy over the years. The football club had changed beyond all recognition, 85 Cowley Hill was now far too big for us and the whole area had lost its small community feel. Whenever I return there I get a similar feeling as I used to when visiting Millwall. It seems all closed in, more bustling and with the single lane two-way system through the centre of the town there is a continual stream of traffic.

Our House in Cowley Hill - 1998

After nearly twelve years in Shoeburyness looking out to sea we are wondering where our next move will be. Back to Boreham Wood? We don't think so. Although I would like to spend more time at the Museum.

As I have already mentioned, I met my wife to be through working at Keystones. I noticed her the first week I was there but was told by a few that I had no chance as she was courting a handsome soldier. I thought, right, R.A.F. v. Squaddie.

Over the next four months or so I kept showing an interest by always being there whenever we went out in groups, by inviting her to my 21st Birthday party and by making sure that when I did start shift work after my training period was over I was on the same shift.

The breakthrough came Xmas Eve 1948. We were on early shift but knocked off at 12.30 pm to go to the Crown Pub for the lunchtime session. Walking home along Shenley Road together about 3.00 pm I asked if she was going back to the Crown that evening to the dance with some of the Keystone girls as I was meeting some of the lads there who also had their eye on one or two of the girls. She replied that she was so I said, *"Right, I will meet you at the top of Clarendon Road at 7.30 pm and we can walk up together"*. Result! She lived first house past the few shops in Shenley Road, just before Meadow Road.

After a meal and a sleep I just managed to get to the shops before they closed to buy a box of smellies, which my Mum wrapped up for me; I am still hopeless at wrapping presents. I remember I gave the present to her in the doorway of McNaughtons, the Chemist shop just before the Dufay Hall, for which I received a peck on the cheek. When we walked into the Crown together a few eyebrows were raised.

As Xmas Day that year was on a Saturday we had four full days off over the Xmas so did not see her again until Wednesday, 28th December at work. We were both at three parties over the New Year either by design or accident and I walked her home each time, and the goodnight kisses got more numerous. The week ending Friday, 7th January we were on late shift, the toppers finished at 10.00 pm and we carried on until midnight. She came down to my machine just after 10.00 pm and told me that she had decided to tell her then boyfriend that it was over. *"Was I still interested?"* I replied, *"Could be, see you tomorrow night"* and that was that.

We continued working at Keystones and for our last two years there we were on opposite shifts. Our wedding date was set for 30th August 1952. Just six weeks before the wedding we were both made redundant from Keystones. Fortunately we both found jobs. Thelma at Standard Telephones and me as an electronic wireman at Elliotts, but our wages were half what we had been earning at Keystones.

We were allocated a Council House in Crown Road August 1953 and while there had two children, Christopher November 1957 and Amanda February 1965. We moved to Cowley Hill 1969 and then to Shoeburyness in 1997. Amanda lives in Suffolk on the Norfolk border and has two children, George and Laura. Christopher lives in Tring in Hertfordshire and has two ready made children, Lee and Kelly. We see them all quite regularly, but not enough.

If we can both make it to 2012 we shall be able to watch the Olympics and celebrate our Diamond Wedding!

I have often thought, no doubt like thousands more, where and how would I have ended up if it had not been for the War?

If I could turn the clock back and have the choice of the unknown or as it turned out, I would without doubt choose the latter.

KEYSTONE FOOTBALL TEAM 1948 - 1949

Back Row
John Juett   Bill O'Neill   Les Farnham John Bentley   Eric Potts   Vic Steele
Front Row
Frank Goodwin   Johnny Oliver   Alan Paley   Peter Woods   Bill Crosland

One of the first games to be played at Eldon Avenue, the new home of
Boreham Wood Football Club   1948

WEDDING DAY

August 30th 1.00pm.
Just Married by Rev. Maddock at
All Saints Church Boreham Wood .
(I could have made it to the Arsenal game !)

Thelma with her sister-in-law, Jean

(photographs - Bill O'Neill)

ADDENDA

The Church Hall - Later called the Village Hall

List of Shops and other premises in Shenley Road about 1941

- Introductory Notes

- Shenley Road North Side from the Crown to Meadow Park

- Shenley Road South Side from Bullens to the Railway Station

Shop Advertisements from All Saints' Church Magazines 1941

The list of shops was sent to me by my old friend Jim Read; see Introduction at the front of the book.

Like myself, Jim came to Boreham Wood in 1941 as a result of being bombed out of his home in East London. The list is based on his memory of the road at that time.

During the course of the War, a number of the shops were taken over by the Government for war purposes. This included light industry, food offices etc. and a few by new proprietors, while others became empty.

The list gives a good indication of the types of shops that plied their wares in most small town high streets at that time.

THE CHURCH or 'Village' HALL

I have recently been informed that the old Church Hall is about to be demolished; for me and no doubt many more it holds very special memories of our youth and the War years. It has always been red in colour and has not changed in appearance over the past sixty-seven years in my knowledge.

Before the War the *Boreham Rovers Football Club* used it for training purposes on Thursday evenings.

At the outbreak of war it became a First Aid Post, Mr Berry being the Chief Warden there and my brother Tom became a regular customer re cut head twice, split lip from a cricket bat, badly cut knees falling off the big swing in Clarendon Park and cut toes stepping on a razor blade in his bare feet one Sunday morning when I was making model aeroplanes. I suffered a clip round the ear from Mum.

When the A.R.P. moved out it became a British Restaurant where for one shilling (5p) you could obtain a basic three course meal (Monday – Friday lunch times only). The kitchens were in the same place as now (2010) and the entrance was down the side nearest the shops.

Almost throughout the War and for quite a few years after, there were always Saturday night dances held there and many a romance began in the old church hall.

Many local weddings were held there plus flower shows, bring and buy sales, jumble sales and various meetings by various organisations in the district. The Boreham Wood Football Club held its inaugural AGM there June 1948.

I and many others spent many happy hours in the Church Hall and at times "enjoyed" some of the Saturday night punch ups. The "dance floor" was just bare boards so plenty of French chalk was used and very often when taking your socks off you could see the shoe line in chalk on your foot.

I would say that the *Church Hall* holds more memories for the people of Boreham Wood (1925-1975) than any other building in the *village* as it was then.

The hall behind the Church Hall did not seem to be used much. I only remember ever going to one dance or social meeting in there and finished up playing the piano. I think it was used more for meetings by various organisations.

Studio Cinema Shenley Road Early 1950s.

(photograph- Derek Allen)

The Dutch Oven on the corner of Grosvenor Road
and the Cock and Hen Club in the 1940s

(photograph- Elstree & Boreham Wood Museuml)

SHOPS & PREMISES IN SHENLEY ROAD CIRCA 1941

NORTH SIDE GOING TOWARDS THE ELSTREE WAY

The Crown Hotel	Tenants Mr & Mrs Morrison, later Bob Moss, later Mr Griffiths
The Crown Off Licence	Closed
Barclays Bank	
Kings	Wet Fish shop
Hastwells	Ironmongers
Presseys	Miss Presseys clothes shop
GLENHAVEN AVENUE	
EJ Freestones	Bakers, the Dutch Oven top shop
Lears Dairy	
Empty Shop	Formerly Pentecosts greengrocers, later Charringtons Coal Office
Thornily Car Showroom	Occupied by W Andrews, Bryce and Furzehill Laboratories. It later became a shopping arcade.
The Post Office	Large stand alone building
The Poplars	A large manor type house occupied by the Royal Corps of Signals
Dufay Chromex Factory	
Tom Wingates Store	Later Miriad Stores
MacNaughtons	Chemist
The Spot Café	
Co-op Grocers	
Barbers Shop	
Co-op Butchers	
Clothes shop	On the corner of the service road to the shops
North Met Showrooms & Offices	Stand alone building
Clintons the Barbers	At the alley entrance to three cottages
Tuckers Haberdashery	On the other side of the Alleyway
Gillham's Greengrocers	Later became Reads
Hanson's	Shop and Tea-rooms
Entrance to Keystones and Furzehill Laboratories	
Central Garage	Owned by Mr Binoth
Then a row of cottages	Isbill the dentist in the first one, with the bus checking clock in front of it.
Mason Estate Agents	A small stand alone white single storey building
Then a row of three storey houses	In one Barkers the cobbler and the last one Doctor Winter.
CLARENDON ROAD	
Elm Farm Dairy	Stand alone building
Open land	Fenced off and housing rabbits owned by Gerrards the Greengrocers, later some of the land housed the nursery
Williams Bros. Grocers	Stand alone building, if you look closely you can still see the slight difference in the brickwork of the original building.
Open land	Fenced off and housed chickens owned by EJ Freestones
The Dutch Oven	Bakery, restaurant and shop. Also Jean's Ladies dress shop
GROSVENOR ROAD	

Open land	Fenced off and housing ducks owned by EJ Freestones; now Barclays Bank
Cock and Hen Club	Owned and run by Freddie Reynolds who lived in Beech Drive
W.V.S. shop or similar	Later Hirsch Tailors
Two small shops	
Gents Hairdresser	Owned by Bob Pratt but run by two Jewish lads while Bob was in the Army (Betting Office and black market goods always available until Bob's return)
Molly's Café	Albert Simmons and Molly. Corned beef, chips, tea and slice of bread one shilling (5p). Albert also ran a café in the A.B.P.C. Studios for the soldiers
Rowlands	Newsagent and Tobacconist when they had any
ELDON AVENUE	All Eldon Avenue had was the white maisonettes as now and was the entrance to the sewage farm further down. The service road between what is now Barclays Bank and Eldon Avenue corner shop was an unmade road with a large oak tree outside of the Cock and Hen Club
Red Lion Hotel	Now McDonalds, the licensees at the time were Fred and Molly Welch; was later taken over by Fred Ainsworth along with his wife and two daughters, Freda and Joyce. Freda married Vincent O'Farrell, a barman, and took over the pub when her dad moved up to take over the Elstree Way Hotel. Freda and Vince left the Red Lion and took over the Seven Bells Pub in Stanmore. John Spence then became landlord, followed by Tom Monahan and then Alf Bartle, who moved to a pub in Stevenage.
Harley House	Shenley Road then turned left before the roundabout was built, then straightened out, On the bend was a large house which later became Harley House,
The Old Firm Café	Run by Ada and Bob Paine. The entrance to the rear of the properties led to two small cottages
Schuftons House	Taken over by Furzehill Laboratories. The automatic pilot was invented here. In 1947 it was taken to Farnborough in a van driven by Jim Read who at the time was working for a road transport delivery firm. It was put into a York aircraft and tested out on a trip to Singapore; not a lot of people know that. When I was given this bit of information by Jim Read in January 2007 it made me remember back to 1947 when I flew back from Germany in a York aircraft carrying out various tests on the way to return to No 218 M.U. a receive test and despatch unit, my home base station in Colerne, Wiltshire where we had a *bit of trouble* on landing. A replacement York aircraft arrived on which we carried out the full test programme. On being signed off it went I know not where within hours of handover. I think the coincidence is too great to even consider.
Studio Cinema	Managed by Mister Culley and his dog Jack. In charge of the ticket office throughout the War and for a long time afterwards was the formidable "Freda Hambrook" who lived in Thrift Farm.

Hedges Yard	Next to the Cinema was Hedges Yard
Single storey building	Housing the London Co-operative Store
Old Church	Catholic Church and Hall
Gates Yard	
A large field	Later became the British Legion Club.
Four Shops	First one was a Grocers shop
	Mr Byers' Sweet and Tobacconist shop
	Greengrocers
Semi-detached houses	Stretching to Meadow Park
	Entrance to Meadow Park Playing Fields

During the War and for a few years after, late spring, summer and early autumn from about 5.30 pm in the evening, Meadow Road Playing Fields, as they were called then, would have dozens of lads of all ages in various groups playing football on any space available, sometimes if your group got there a bit late it would be difficult to find a space for your kick around. It was where we learnt our football. If the Council had not taken the goal posts down from the previous Saturday's game it was a bonus. There would be two groups, one either side of the goal with two keepers almost back to back.

As the years went by dog walkers and the odd golfer took over, the youth of the time much preferring to hang around in aimless groups bored out of their minds.

After the War the Boreham Rovers resumed playing football on Meadow Road Playing Fields, now Meadow Park, on the identical spot where the all-weather surface is today. A year later the Royal Retournez F.C. played on a pitch at right angles to the Rovers alongside the old tennis courts until the amalgamation in 1948 when they moved to Eldon Avenue. They then moved back to their present ground August 1963.

The tower block flats now stand on one goal area of the Eldon Avenue ground and the BBC Television Studios, formerly ATV, on the other goal area. The Eastenders set is on what was one of the backfields.

At the end of the 1947/48 Football season I became involved with the Boreham Wood Football Club and became a founder member of the present club when they amalgamated with the Royal Retournez F.C. in June 1948.

This part of my life is well chronicled in my book which was published in 2005 entitled *"From Meadow Road to Meadow Park via Eldon Avenue"*. To date I am still President of the Club and in my 63rd year with the Club, something that I am very proud of.

SHOPS & PREMISES IN SHENLEY ROAD CIRCA 1941

SOUTH SIDE GOING TOWARDS THE RAILWAY STATION

Bullens	Storage and Removals
A.B.P.C. Studios	The studio buildings stood way back with a large lawn in front of them with a high hawthorn hedge along the road frontage Now a Tesco Supermarket
Grosvenor Hotel	Then a hotel and milk bar until Josef and Myra took it over and opened the restaurant
Acasons	Newsagents
Cleavers	Grocers
Victoria Wine Co.	Off Licence
WHITEHOUSE AVENUE	
Bakers Shop	Bob Freestone
Bonds	Wet Fish Shop
	The building line then went back 2/3 feet; can still be seen
Four empty shops	Taken over by Simpsons Transformers
Open space	VE night bonfire site. You can see where the additional shops were built on
CARDINAL AVENUE	Cardinal Avenue had privet hedges up both sides on the kerb edge; luckily horses do not eat privet hedge
The Kiosk	London Tobacco Company
Sainsburys	
Boots	Chemist
Meyers	Greengrocers
Paynes	Florist
Bentley's	Furniture shop
Empty shop	Labour Exchange transferred here from Theobald Street
The Church Hall	Later a British Restaurant
The Vicarage	The Reverend Maddocks
All Saints Church	
Two houses	Harold Starck, the taxi man, lived in one
Entrance way	To the Elstree Rural District Council Offices. All single storey buildings.
Four houses	The first one was Beatties Photographers, later Dr. Longman moved his surgery into one.
The Baptist Church	With a large lawn down to Furzehill Road and a high privet hedge around it
FURZEHILL ROAD	
Large empty shop	Later Lilleys Electrical Shop, then the Heating Centre.
Kilbys	The Grocers
Cherrys	Boot and Shoe Repairers
Mr & Mrs Clark's house	Nobby, the son, worked at Keystones
Annie Byers	Sweet Shop
A house	
Hunts the Butchers	Later Pauline Miller's Dance School, then hairdressers
DRAYTON ROAD	
Empty shop	
Ann Chessall	Baby Wear Shop
Shop	W.V.S.
Wilkins	Shoe Shop

Large orchard	Stretched back to the Challenge Works at the bottom of Drayton Road
National Provincial Bank	You can see "the join" between what was Wilkins Shoe Shop, four up from Drayton Road, and where the old Provincial Bank building still is to give some idea of the size of the orchard
Elstree Radio Shop	Selling radios etc. and bicycles owned by Mr Allison
Grooms	Men's Wear
Alleyway between shops	
Kidwells	Newsagents
Two or three empty shops	
Westminster Bank	
STATION ROAD	Down to the Gate Studios, the Gas Works and Gas House Lane cottages on the right, on the left was the public toilets which before the War was a small cinema.
THEOBALD STREET or RADLETT ROAD, East Side	Behind the Crown car park, The Old Crown which became a coal merchants then Don Roberts Builders Merchants. There was the Wellington Pub run by Olive, Bonds Wet Fish Shop, an empty shop before the alleyway that went to Glenhaven Avenue, Tompkins butcher's shop, and Bob Freestone's with bakery at the rear.
THEOBALD STREET West Side	Breathwaites Furniture and Upholsterers, the old slaughterhouse and the Working Men's Club

There were not many *shopping shops* as such and most people went by bus to Burnt Oak and Watford.

I do not remember there being a fish and chip shop in Boreham Wood during the War.

The only other shops I can remember in the district were a general store in Well End, a few shops in Elstree Village and a few in Shenley.

No doubt there will be a few queries raised on some of the shops named but we are talking about over sixty-five years ago.

The difference between then and today is that you knew many of the shop owners and their families, also those that served in the shops. You also met people you knew and you spent more time *gossiping* than shopping, you kept in touch with what was going on specially on births, deaths and marriages.

Also in those days many more people had their milk and bread delivered, and also quite a few had their meat from the butchers. Everything was much more personal and I believe that because we all knew each other the street crime did not happen, unlike today. In those days the police, school teachers, parents and grown ups were respected.

Local Traders Advertisements 1941

Telephone: 1185.

Purveyors of High-Class Dairy Produce.

Elm Farm Dairy

(Proprietor LEONARD COOK)

125, SHENLEY ROAD

All Milk supplied from local Farms

And at ELSTREE.

UNDER PERSONAL SUPERVISION.

Caterer & Pastrycook.

Phone: 1161

The "Dutch Oven"

(PROPRIETOR R. J. FREESTONE)

SHENLEY ROAD

AND AT

HIGH STREET

For Dainty Teas.

KILBY'S STORES

High Class
GROCERS & PROVISION
MERCHANTS.

The Store for Quality and Value.

BACON our Speciality

SHENLEY ROAD.

Telephone: 1197.

W. H. STEVENS,

Coal and Coke Merchant

Office: 27 MALDEN ROAD,

Yard: GLEN HAVEN AVENUE.

Phone: 1701.

Expert advice on all matters of Domestic Fires.

H. J. HASTWELL, UNDERTAKER,

Shenley Road.

Phone: 1033.

A Selection of Local Traders Advertisements from 1941 Issues of All Saints Magazines

The Grosvenor Restaurant and Café where Nanny Marsh worked when we came to Boreham Wood